Our Great Seal

OurGREAT SEAL

THE SYMBOLS OF OUR HERITAGE AND OUR DESTINY

By

E. Raymond Capt M.A., A.I.A., F.S.A. Scot.
Archaeological Institute of America

Revised and Expanded

PUBLISHED BY

ARTISAN PUBLISHERS
1409 West Shawnee
Muskogee, OK 74401

ISBN 0-934666-00-8
Library of Congress catalog card number: 79-53862

To ''Mark'' and other members of the
United States Armed Forces who paid
the price of Liberty and Freedom with
wounded bodies and broken minds.

PREFACE

The Great Seal of the United States of America is the symbol of our Nation's Independence. Its design constitutes our National Arms. As the National Arms, the Seal states symbolically the principles which animated the founders of our Republic. Today those principles are being forgotten. Because they are being neglected, America is fast losing sight of the two greatest forces that motivated our Founding Fathers – Christianity and Patriotism. From these two principles sprang our national constitutional laws, freedom of speech and worship, equality and fraternity.

Without Christianity and Patriotism, America can lose her place of leadership in the family of nations – perhaps, even her freedom. To avert that danger, we must go back to the fundamentals of true Americanism clearly set forth in the symbolism of the Great Seal of the United States. America has a Destiny, and to fully understand this Destiny one must recognize that our nation and its armorial insignia were not evolved by chance.

A "Code of Arms" of a family or a nation is never taken lightly. Much thought is given to the design, and every detail is considered at length: the rich traditions of the past, the hopes of the future, ancestry, and Faith. All these things and more play a part in its design. The Great Seal of the United States is no exception. Its emblazoned facts bristle with symbolic significance. Symbolism is not only natural and general, but Christ Himself taught by symbols – to quote the Scriptures, ". . . *without a parable* [or symbol] *spake he not unto them.*"

Our ancestors chose emblems for our Coat of Arms that were natural and of immediate significance to them, as well as their hopes for the future. They envisoned a "New World Order" based on the principles of Christian brotherhood, where all men have equal rights to "life, liberty and the pursuit of happiness." They planned well and wisely and were undoubtedly influenced to no small degree (whether they knew it or not) by the All-wise, overruling Divine Providence.

GLOSSARY

The following glossary of heraldic terms are used in the description of the Great Seal of the United States of America.

Argent	– silver or white
Armorial achievement	– a (whole) coat of arms
Azure	– blue
Banded	– encircled with a band or riband
Bearing	– applicable to any single charge or heraldic device
Charges	– the bearings and emblems of Heraldry
Chief	– upper part of a shield, occupying one-third thereof
Crest	– an ornament for the head
Dexter	– right hand side of the design (not of the observer)
Displayed	– applied to any bird of prey with its wings expanded
Escutcheon	– shield
Field	– whole surface of the escutcheon or shield upon which the charges or bearings are depicted
Glory	– a series of rays surrounding or issuing from a charge or ordinary (a common bearing bounded by straight lines)
Gules	– red
Motto	– a word, saying or sentence borne on a scroll under the coat of arms and sometimes over the crest
Or	– metal gold
Paleway (Paly)	– bands placed vertically on the face of a shield
Pileus	– cap of Liberty
Proper	– applicable to all animals, trees, vegetables, etc., when borne of their natural color
Scroll	– one of the ornaments which may accompany the shield, usually bearing a motto
Sinister	– left hand side of the design (not of the observer)
Supporter	– a figure of a living creature (although it may be mythical) represented as holding up or standing beside the shield

DEFINITION OF A "SEAL"

Webster's New World Dictionary defines (in part) a "seal":

1. A design, initial, or other device placed on a letter, document, etc., as a signature or proof of authenticity; letters were formerly closed with a wafer of molten wax into which was pressed the distinctive seal of the sender.
2. A stamp, signet ring, etc. used for making such an impression.
3. A wax wafer, piece of paper, etc., bearing the impression of some design recognized, usually by law, as official.

In general practice, a "seal" consists of three parts:

1. Any block or piece of hard material (stone, metal, etc.), incised with a device, figure, symbol, or the like, in such manner that it can, with the application of pressure, impart an impression in relief on a plastic substance, such as wax, moistened clay, or paper.
2. An impression so made.
3. The substance bearing the impression.

In other words, a "seal" is any one, or all, of three things:

1. The engraved die used to make the impression.
2. The impression made from it.
3. The wax, clay, paper, or other material on which the impression had been made.

SEAL OF ALEXANDER DE BALLIOL, A.D. 1292

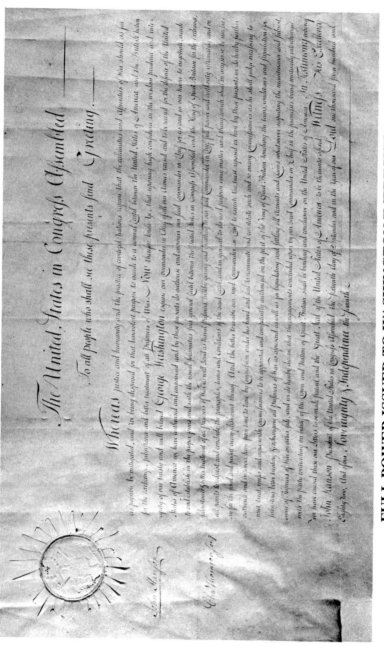

FULL POWER ISSUED TO WASHINGTON IMPRESSED WITH THE FIRST DIE (1782)

The significance of a seal is that it implies a deliberate and considered act on the part of him who affixes it. It serves to identify, in the same manner as a signature, an individual, organization, or other entity, and to authenticate written matter emanating therefrom. The matter engraved on the die and forming the device of the seal may be an emblem, symbol, heraldic bearing, letter or letters, word or words, or any other identifying mark or design.

A "Great Seal" is the principal seal of a nation, state, or other major political entity, used for authenticating documents of high importance or high ceremony issued in the name of the sovereign or chief executive authority. Generally, Great Seals are of the wafer (paper) type attached to the face of the document. It may be impressed directly on the page of the document, without the use of a paper wafer, as authorized by the act of Congress approved May 31, 1854. (10 Stat. 297, 1 U.S. Code 114)

Legally, as well as in general usage, the Seal has two equally correct designations: "the Seal of the United States" and "the Great Seal." Both designations are to be found in acts of Congress and in a decision of the Supreme Court. The Congressional Act of September 15, 1789 (which changed the Department of Foreign Affairs to the Department of State) places the Seal in the custody of the Secretary of State and requires that it be affixed: ". . . to all civil commissions, for officers of the United States, to be appointed by the President, by and with the advice and consent of the Senate, or by the President alone. Provided that the said seal shall not be affixed to any commission, before the same shall have been signed by the President of the United States, nor to any other instrument or act, without the special warrant of the President therefor."

The use of seals can be traced back to the earliest periods of history – 4000 B.C. or earlier. They are mentioned in the Bible. Judah, the son of Jacob, left his "seal" as a pledge with Tamar *"whom he did not know."* Josephus records, and so do the Scriptures, how the Thessalonians wrote a letter of friendship to the Judeans and claimed them as brethren in Abraham, sealing their letter with the "seal" of Dan, their father, as testimony. (The generic name of the Greeks was "Danai" – and their true origin is as much a mystery as that of the "Tuatha De Danaans" of Ireland, whose prince was married by Jeremiah the Prophet to the daughter of King Zedekiah of Judah – See *Jacob's Pillar* by Capt – listed inside rear cover.)

Each of the tribes of Israel had its individual standard, and the patriarch of the tribe wore its signet (seal). The devices upon them

3

were taken from the symbology of the blessings pronounced upon the heads of their fathers (Gen. 49; Deut. 33:7-25). In Tabernacle days, Aaron, the High Priest, wore a gold plate upon which was engraved a "seal": *"And thou shalt make a plate of pure gold, and grave upon it, like the engravings of a signet, HOLINESS TO THE LORD. And thou shalt put it on a blue lace, that it may be upon the mitre; upon the forefront of the mitre it shall be."* (Exod. 28:36,37)

At this point it should be noted that in describing the symbolism of the Great Seal and its relationship to America we will be using the words "Israel" and "Israelitish." In doing so, it will be helpful to bear in mind that in the Scriptures the terms "Israel," "Judah," and "Jew" are not synonymous, and the course of history is widely divergent for the peoples properly classified under each of these titles. In describing the various devices incorporated in the Great Seal as having "Israelitish" origins, we do not mean "Jewish." What is meant is that the "Israelitish" symbols can be traced back to the 12 tribes of Israel who came out of Egypt under the command of Moses. Judaism originated, centuries later, with a remnant of the tribe of Judah during their Babylonian captivity.

Although for centuries Christendom has followed the practice of calling all the descendants of Jacob (whose name was changed to "Israel"), "Jews," the term can only properly apply to the small remnant of the Israel tribe of Judah, who, with a mixture of Babylonians, returned to Jerusalem from Babylon in the time of Ezra and Nehemiah. The Encyclopaedia Britannica, quoting a Jewish professor of Hebrew, defines the word Jew: "The word Jew . . . occurring only in the latter parts of the Old Testament and signifying a descendant of Judah, the fourth son of Jacob, whose tribe – together with that of his half-brother Benjamin – constituted the Kingdom of Judah, as opposed to that of the remaining tribes (Israel). The name came to mean the followers of Judaism, including in-born and proselytes, the racial signification diminishing as the religious increased."

One further elaboration of the definition should be made. The term "Great Seal" implies the existence of a lesser seal. The expression is believed to have originated in England during the reign of King John (1155-1216). For the sovereign's private business a "privy seal" was acquired. This seal was of smaller size and in recognition of the contrast between the two, the large seal used on documents of state soon became known as the "Great Seal." Since, in the United States,

THE LION AND THE UNICORN

The British Coat of Arms depicts the Lion and the Unicorn, the young lions, the Harp of David and the scarlet thread of Zarah – all Israel symbols, and the motto translated means "God and my (birth)right."

THOMAS JEFFERSON PRESENTING HIS DRAFT OF THE DECLARATION OF INDEPENDENCE

the Great Seal serves the purpose parallel with that of the British Great Seal, the term was adopted. However, the United States has no lesser seal comparable to the British privy seal.

HISTORY OF THE GREAT SEAL

It was late in the afternoon of July 4, 1776, after the members of the Continental Congress had signed the "Declaration of Independence," that a resolution was passed: "Resolved, that Dr. Franklin, Mr. J. Adams and Mr. Jefferson be a committee to prepare a device for a seal of the United States of America." The committee was the same as had drawn up the Declaration of Independence, except for the omission of Robert Livingston and Rodger Sherman.

The purpose for wanting a seal was to complete the evidence of the act of Independence, by formally adopting an official Sign of Sovereignty and a National Coat of Arms. The several colonies each had a seal, generally simple but significant. These could have served as patterns for a seal, but the members of the committee were guided by a desire to illustrate, in an allegorical picture, the fortunes and destiny of the United States as a whole.

As none of the members of the committee could draw, they engaged the services of an artist and writer, Eugene Pierre Du Simitiere, a West Indian Frenchman who lived in Philadelphia. Born in Geneva, Switzerland (1737), De Simitiere became a naturalized citizen in New York in 1769. He was an avid student of every aspect of American history, collecting books, pamphlets, newspapers, hand-bills, and every other kind of political publication. He strove to record the history of the Colonies and their struggles for independence. All the while, he continued to practice his profession of artist and painter, and was called upon to draw designs for a variety of State, local and institutional seals.

The committee consulted among themselves between July 4th and August 13th, and each submitted a proposal for a device. We read of Du Simitiere's suggestion for the design of the Seal in "Familiar Letters of John Adams to His Wife": "(Du Simitiere) . . . a painter by profession, whose designs are very ingenious, and his drawings well executed. He has been applied to for his advice. I waited on him yesterday, and saw his sketches . . . For the seal he proposes the arms of the several nations from whence America has been peopled; as English, Scotch, Irish, Dutch, German, etc., each in a shield. On one side of them, Liberty with her pileus (cap), on the other a rifler in his uniform, with his rifled-gun in one hand and his tomahawk in the other. This dress and these troops with the kind of armor being peculiar to America – unless the dress was known to the Romans . . ."

OBVERSE
PENCIL SKETCH BY DU SIMITIERE,
FOUND IN THE JEFFERSON PAPERS

Ideas for the design of the reverse seal were made by members of the committee, and it is quite significant that most of their ideas or suggestions bore Israelitish symbols. In John Adams' letters we find the following remarks: ". . . Dr. F. proposes a device for a seal: Moses lifting up his hand dividing the Red Sea, and Pharaoh in his chariot overwhelmed with the waters. This motto, 'Rebellion to Tyrants is Obedience to God.' Mr. Jefferson proposed: the children of Israel in the Wilderness, led by a cloud by day and a pillar of fire by night; on the other side, Hengist and Horsa, the Saxon chiefs from whom we claim the honor of being descended, and whose political principles and form of government we have assumed."

Corroboration of Adams' report is found in the notes preserved by Jefferson and now among his papers in the Library of Congress. It reads: "Pharaoh sitting in an open chariot, a crown on his head and a sword in his hand passing thro' the divided waters of the Red Sea in pursuit of the Israelites; rays from a pillar of fire in the cloud, expressive of the divine presence and command, reaching to Moses who stands on the shore and, extending his hand over the sea, causes it to overwhelm Pharaoh. Motto, Rebellion to tyrants is obed. . ."

Jefferson's notes detail Franklin's design of the Children of Israel crossing the Red Sea: "Moses standing on the shore, and extending his hand over the sea, thereby causing the same to overwhelm Pharaoh, who is sitting in an open chariot, a crown on his head and a sword in his hand; rays from a Pillar of Fire in the clouds reaching to Moses to express that he acts by Command of the Deity. Motto, Rebellion to tyrants is obedience to God."

In one of the most remarkable chapters in our history, Jefferson and Franklin, both freethinkers, proposed designs having to do with Israelitish symbols taken from the Bible. Commenting upon the suggestions of this first Committee, Professor Charles A. L. Totten (see page 99) wrote: "A general point of interest upon the Great Seal is the unanimity with which they went to the Scriptures as the fountain source of the most glowing symbolism. The early struggles toward liberty of the Hebrew people with tyrannical Egypt – the land of bricks without straw – was most naturally suggestive of our own struggles with the mother country, then trying, like the Pharaoh of old, to exact from us a toll of taxation without representation. As the passage of the Red Sea had been prepared for the escape of Israel, so the broad Atlantic had been smoothed for the Pilgrims as they fled through the sea into the wilderness beyond, which was to be their 'desolate heritage,' this later people – set apart for greater purposes. So, too, the hardened ruler of Old England essayed to pursue across the ocean and into the farther wilderness beyond, only to encounter equivalent destruction."

The first Committee's report to Congress (August 20, 1776) contained, but modified, Du Simitiere's suggestions for the Obverse of the Seal. The center Shield was divided into six quarters, containing the symbols of the six principal countries from which the American colonists had come: The Rose of England, the Thistle of Scotland, the Harp of Ireland, the Fleur de Lis of France, the Eagle of Germany, and the Lion of Holland. The Shield was supported by the Goddess of Justice and the Goddess of Liberty. The Goddess of Liberty, originally resting her left hand on an anchor (which was omitted), was altered to use the hand to support the shield. The Goddess of Justice (replacing the rifler) bears a "Sword" in her right hand, and in her left a "Balance." The whole was surrounded by a border, containing 13 small shields, with the initials of the 13 original states. Above the Shield was placed a "Radiant Triangle" with the "Eye of Providence" in the center. For the Reverse seal, the committee's report recommended Franklin's design with some changes by Jefferson.

REVERSE

OBVERSE

DRAWING BY BENSON J. LOSSING (1856)
OF DESIGNS REPORTED BY THE FIRST COMMITTEE

The Journals of the Continental Congress (V, 691) record the fate of the first committee's report in these words: "Ordered, to be on the table." Then, as now, in Congress, this action had the effect of killing the proposal. Although the original report has been lost and no reason can be found for the action taken, it is evident that the majority of Congress were dissatisfied with the design.

On March 25, 1780, Congress, responding to a growing need for a seal device, appointed a second committee. The members named to this committee were James Lowell of Massachusetts (Chairman), John Morin Scott of New York, and William Churchill Houston of New Jersey. The committee acquired the services of Francis Hopkinson, who had previously been a member of the Continental Congress. Hopkinson was noted for his interest and knowledge of heraldry. In 1776, he had designed, or helped design, the Great Seal of New Jersey. He also was noted for having designed the American flag that Congress adopted on June 14, 1777.

So far as the records show, Hopkinson, with the help of clerical assistance, did most of the work of this committee. He prepared two sets of drawings or sketches, each consisting of an obverse and a reverse. Both sets are generally similar but with noticeable differences. For the obverse in both sets he used the shield with a military figure and a female figure as supporters (from the first committee's report). The differences were the addition of fifteen white and red diagonal stripes, which filled the shield between the supporters in the first sketch; and thirteen stripes with a blue field in the corners, above and below, in the second.

Other differences between the two obverse designs are to be noted. The first set has as its dexter (right) supporter a "naked savage" holding a bow and arrow in his right hand and carrying a quiver of arrows on his back; whereas the second has a soldier, in what appears to be antiquated clothing, with a drawn sword in his right hand. The motto of the first is "Bello vel Pace Paratus," whereas the second is "Bello vel Paci." Both obverses have, above the shields, a constellation of thirteen six-pointed stars; the first somewhat smaller than the second. The stars, as well as the white and red stripes used on the shield, undoubtedly were inspired by the American flag which Congress had adopted on June 14, 1777.

**HOPKINSON'S DRAWING OF HIS FIRST PROPOSAL
FOR THE OBVERSE**

**HOPKINSON'S DRAWING OF HIS REVISED PROPOSAL
FOR THE OBVERSE**

**HOPKINSON'S DRAWING OF HIS FIRST PROPOSAL
FOR THE REVERSE**

**HOPKINSON'S DRAWING OF HIS REVISED PROPOSAL
FOR THE REVERSE**

For the reverses, Hopkinson uses a female figure, representing Liberty, as the basic device. Several differences between the two sets can also be noted. In the first, the figure of Liberty holds a sword in her left hand; in the second, an olive branch. In the first, the motto in the upper part of the circle reads, "Aut Haec aut Nullus"; in the second, "Semper," which is crossed out and "Libertas Virtute perennis" written above the circle. In the first, the date at the bottom is "MDCCLXXX"; in the second, "MDCCLXXVI."

On May 17, 1780, Congress considered the report, debated it, and ordered it back to the committee for further study. Although additional work was done on the Seal, Congress took no further action on the second committee's report. During the following year, Congress passed several resolutions relating to the Seal, and on January 28, 1782, they passed a resolution specifying certain duties of the Secretary of Congress. Among the duties was the following:

"6th. To keep the public seal, and cause the same to be affixed to every act, ordinance or paper, which Congress shall direct": (Journals, XXII, 56-57).

Since there was then no Great Seal, the need of another committee was recognized by Congress. A third committee was appointed on May 2, 1782. This committee consisted of Elias Boudinot of New Jersey (then President of Congress) and Arthur Middleton and Edward Rutledge of South Carolina. The committee called into consultation William Barton, an authority on Heraldry and the son of Rev. Thomas Barton, Rector of St. James Episcopal Church of Philadelphia.

Barton submitted two designs. One of these was illustrated and retained some of the ideas submitted by the preceding committees: the thirteen stars, the blue field, and the thirteen stripes of red and white or white and red. His original contribution to this design was the eagle. At the same time, Barton submitted a design for the reverse face of the Seal. The reverse consisted of an unfinished pyramid of 13 courses of masonry. Over the pyramid was the "Eye of Providence" surrounded by a circle of rays and the motto "Deo Favente," and below the Pyramid the motto "Perennis."

While the reverse design seemed to be acceptable, Congress was not satisfied with the obverse seal. They referred the matter to the

DRAWING BY CONNOR (1976)
OF BARTON'S FIRST PROPOSAL (THIRD COMMITTEE)

15

WILLIAM BARTON'S SECOND DEVICE
(TRACED FROM ORIGINAL)

Secretary of Congress, Charles Thomson. By an order of Congress (June 13, 1782), Thomson was given the final decision on a modification of all previous designs. In effect, Thomson was now a committee of one charged with preparing a design for the seal. With his assignment, Thomson was given all of the reports, drawings, and other pages of the three committees before him.

Thomson promptly set about producing a design of his own. He studied the blazons and sketches of the prior seal committees, giving particular attention to Hopkinson's drawings of his first obverse (see page 12). His major innovations were in placing the American Bald Eagle as the central theme; depicted as rising, not displayed, and placing symbols of peace and war (olive branch and arrows) in the eagle's talons. The olive branch had figured in the design of the second committee but the arrows were used for the first time. From the report of the first committee, he took the motto, "E. Pluribus Unum."

THOMSON'S DRAWING OF HIS PROPOSAL – 1782

Thomson patterned his reverse after Barton's design. Several modifications are noted: the Eye in the Zenith was surrounded by the triangle Barton had omitted; Barton's motto "Deo favente" was replaced by "Annuit Coeptis," and a second motto, "Novus Ordo Seclorum" was added; the year of independence in Roman numerals (from Du Simitiere's design) was added on the base of the pyramid. Thomson made no drawings of his reverse but handed his descriptions and sketches to Barton for final revision.

On June 19, 1782, Barton proceeded to rewrite Thomson's description of the obverse in the precise language of heraldry, including specifications of colors. He made a major change in the design of the shield, substituting for Thomson's chevrons, thirteen pales (vertical stripes) alternately white and red below a blue "chief," or upper part of the shield. He restored the "displayed" eagle (as his original design) and specified that the bundle of arrows held in the eagle's left talon should number thirteen. Describing the crest more specifically, he stipulated that it include thirteen stars. To the whole device he added an exergue and a legend around the margin, both of which were subsequently discarded.

On June 20, 1782, Charles Thomson submitted to Congress his report recommending a design for the Great Seal, and Congress adopted the device the same day. In the "Journals of Congress" there is this record of the report:

"The Secretary of the United States in Congress assembled to whom were referred the several reports of committees on the device for a great seal, to take order, reports

That the Device for an Armorial Achievement & Reverse of the great seal for the United States in Congress assembled is as follows:

Arms

Paleways of thirteen pieces Argent and Gules: a Chief, Azure, The Escutcheon on the breast of the American Bald Eagle displayed, proper, holding in his dexter talon an Olive branch, and in his sinister a bundle of thirteen arrows, all proper, & in his beak a scroll, inscribed with this Motto, 'E. Pluribus unum.'

For the Crest

Over the head of the Eagle which appears above the Escutcheon, A Glory, Or, breaking through a cloud, proper, & surrounding thirteen stars forming a Constellation, Argent, on an Azure field.

Reverse

A pyramid unfinished. In the Zenith an Eye in a triangle surrounded with a glory proper. Over the Eye these words 'Annuit Coeptis.' On the base of the pyramid the numerical letters MDCCLXXVI & underneath the following motto: 'Novus Ordo Seclorum.'"

DRAWING BY BENEDICT (1903)
OF BARTON'S MODIFICATION
OF THOMSON'S PROPOSAL

Also, constituting an essential part of the statute as Congress adopted it but left out of the "Journals of Congress" are these "Remarks and Explanation" in Thomson's handwriting and endorsed by him:

"The Escutcheon is composed of the chief & pale, the two most honorable ordinaries. The Pieces, paly, represent the several states all joined in one solid entire, supporting a Chief, which unites the whole & represents Congress. The Motto alludes to this union. The pales in the arms are kept closely united by the Chief, and the Chief depends on that union & strength resulting from it for its support, to denote the

Confederacy of the United States of America & the preservation of their Union through Congress.

"The colours of the pales are those used in the flag of the United States of America: White signifies purity and innocence; Red, hardiness & valour; and Blue, the colour of the Chief, signifies vigilance, perseverance & justice. The Olive branch and arrows denote the power of peace & war which is exclusively vested in Congress. The Constellation denotes a new State taking its place and rank among other sovereign powers. The Escutcheon is born on the breast of an American Eagle without any other supporters, to denote that the United States ought to rely on their own virtue.

"Reverse. The pyramid signifies Strength and Duration: The Eye over it & the Motto allude to the many signal interpositions of Providence in favour of the American cause. The date underneath is that of the Declaration of Independence and the words under it signify the beginning of the new American Era which commences from that date."

From Thomson's "Remarks and Explanation" it is clear that every device on the Great Seal (obverse and reverse) is symbolic in that it represents another thing. Heraldry, itself, is a language of symbolism. Government publications explain the official intent of the symbolical meanings of the various devices of the Seal; however, students of biblical symbolism suggest that there are other mystical and esoteric meanings hidden in the design of our National Arms. Although such suggestions are not found in the surviving official documentation of the history of the Seal, there is cause to believe that there is a deeply religious and supremely spiritual truth incorporated in the Great Seal. This will become more and more obvious as we proceed to elucidate the symbolism of each device of the Seal.

The first die of the Great Seal, cut in brass in 1782, showed a crested eagle instead of the American bird prescribed by law. Its impress, about 2¼ inches in diameter, is easily identified by the border of modified conventional acanthus leaves, the six-pointed stars, and the fact that the arrows touch the border. It was usually impressed on a circular paper wafer attached to the document by a disk of red adhesive. This brought out the device in relief at the same time that it held the wafer to the document. The original die of 1782 is on permanent display in the National Archives.

THE GREAT DIE OF 1782

IMPRESSION FROM THE DIE OF 1782

On May 5, 1825, a steel die measuring $4^{11}/_{16}$ inches in diameter and $1^{1}/_{4}$ inches in thickness was cut by Seraphim Masi, a jeweler and silversmith of Washington, D.C. The device depicts the eagle realistically rather than heraldically. It also departs from the description contained in the resolution of 1782 by omitting from the upper part of the shield and from the crest the horizontal lines that in heraldic engraving represent azure (blue).

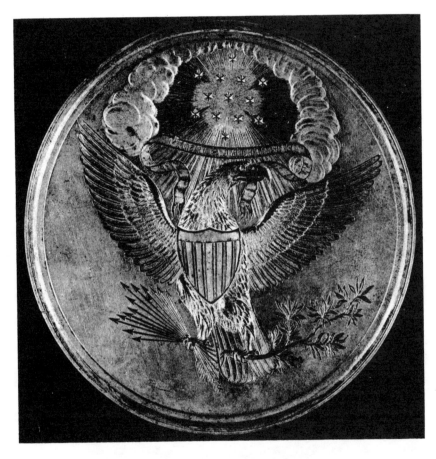

THE MASI TREATY-SEAL DIE OF 1825

Seraphim Masi's seal-die was in service for forty-six years. The die was never, so far as known, impressed otherwise than as a pendant seal. It was usually used on original instruments of ratification of treaties designed for exchange with foreign governments. Thus it became known as the "Masi treaty-seal." The last use of the Masi treaty-seal die of 1825 (and the last pendant seal) was on the instrument of ratification of the Treaty of May 8, 1871, with Great Britain, the famous Treaty of Washington.

IMPRESSION FROM THE DIE OF 1825

A successor to the die of 1782 was cut in cast steel by John V. N. Throop of Washington in 1841. It was about the same size as the first die but distinguishable by the crowding at the top, its very small five-pointed stars, and its sheaf of six instead of thirteen arrows in the eagle's sinister talon. From this characteristic it has been called "the illegal seal," although the legality of the documents to which it was affixed has never been questioned.

THE THROOP DIE OF 1841

Blame for the faulty design of the die has been placed on Daniel Webster, who was Secretary of State at the time it was put into use. However, it is more likely that Throop was not given the text of the resolution of June 20, 1782, setting forth the seal design in heraldic terms and specifying thirteen arrows. If this was the case, he worked solely from an impression from the worn die of 1782 that would have shown a bundle of arrows, but their number may well have been indistinguishable. In like manner, the six-pointed stars in the crest of the die of 1782 became five-pointed stars in the new die, an innovation which has been copied from die to die down to the one in use today.

IMPRESSION FROM THE DIE OF 1841

From 1841 to 1871, the Department of State used, concurrently, the Masi treaty-seal die of 1825 and the Throop die of 1841. During this time the pendant seals were kept in "skippet" or ornamental metal boxes. On the skippet cover, usually in silver or gold, was a replica of the seal in relief. One such skippet, supplied to the Department of State by Samuel Lewis (Washington jeweler and silversmith), was made with a heavy iron silversmith's mold. The replica of the seal on the cover was copied so closely to that of the Masi treaty-seal that impressions from the two are difficult to tell apart.

**THE LEWIS SKIPPET-COVER MOLD,
USED AS A DIE IN 1871**

The Lewis skippet-cover mold did not fully conform to the specifications of the resolutions of June 20, 1782, lacking the horizontal lines to represent blue (azure) in the upper part of the shield and in the background of the stars in the crest; lacking the scattering of dots to represent gold (or) among the rays of glory of the crest. Nevertheless it was impressed on a treaty of commerce and navigation between the United States and Italy (1871). Consequently, the Lewis Mold, intended for making skippet covers, must be counted among the dies actually used for impressing the Great Seal of the United States.

**IMPRESSION FROM
THE LEWIS SKIPPET-COVER MOLD**

In 1877, the Department of State commissioned Herman Baumgarten, a Washington engraver from Germany, to engrave the "Great Seal of the United States in Steel" and construct a "Press" with "Case and Locks." The die was very much like the die of 1841, ignoring the law in regards to the number of arrows, but it had larger stars. As in the case of the 1841 die, no reverse was cut of either of these incorrect seals.

IMPRESSION FROM THE DIE OF 1877

Criticisms of the failure of the 1841 and 1877 dies to conform to the blazon of the law of 1782 led the Secretary of State to ask Congress for an appropriation of $1,000, for the purpose of having a new seal made. On July 7, 1884, Congress passed an act making the appropriation "to enable the Secretary of State to obtain dies of the obverse and reverse of the seal of the United States and the Appliances necessary for making impressions from and for the preservation of the same."

James Horton Whitehouse, chief designer for Tiffany & Co., was given the task of drawing the official versions of the seal as approved by Congress. In December of 1884, his designs were accepted as complying with the description in the law. A die of the obverse, having a diameter of three inches, was cut by Tiffany & Co. in 1885. Although it is commonly believed that no die for the reverse of the seal was cut at that time, there is evidence indicating that such a die may have been cut – though never put into use.

WHITEHOUSE'S PRELIMINARY DRAWING (1884)
FOR THE OBVERSE

The Tiffany die clearly portrays thirteen arrows in the eagle's sinister talon, thereby correcting the error in the number of arrows Throop had introduced in the die of 1841, and which had been perpetuated in the Baumgarten die of 1877. Also, the olive branch is clearly depicted with thirteen leaves and thirteen olives.

A letter written (1893) about the Tiffany die gives the following information: "The (die) . . . of 1885 is cut in the finest steel, and the plate on which the paper is placed to receive the impression is of bronze. The seal die, which is three inches in diameter, with a weight of one pound six ounces, is used in a screw press. By an ingenious mechanism the impression can now be given to show the eagle head up, as in the former press was impossible in the case of bulky documents."

THE TIFFANY DIE OF 1885

By 1902, the die of 1885 had worn down to the extent that Congress appropriated $1,250 for the cutting of a replacement. It was ordered that the new die should reproduce as exactly as possible the design of 1885, thus assuring faithfulness to the law of 1782. The old die was removed from the press and was handed down from one seal custodian to the next, its identity eventually forgotten until it was re-identified in 1976.

IMPRESSION FROM THE DIE OF 1885

The new die was cut in hardened steel by Baily & Biddle of Philadelphia and first used on January 27, 1904. It was cut by an expert engraver in that firm's employ, Max Zeitler. Subsequently, the die is known as the "Zeitler Die of 1904." This die is the Seal in use today. It remains on public view at all times, and with a permanent exhibit of documents allows visitors to see the role of the Seal in the conduct of our country's foreign and domestic affairs. Despite more than 72 years of almost daily use, the die, press, and cabinet of 1904 remain in excellent condition and appear able to provide years of further service.

THE ZEITLER DIE OF 1904

Impressions from Zeitler's die are three inches in diameter and so nearly identical otherwise with impressions from the die of 1885 that it is difficult to tell them apart without close examination. A number of minor stylistic details are noticeable between the new die and the Tiffany die which it replaced: (1) the feathers on the eagle's wings and tail are more pointed than that of 1885; (2) the talons of the eagle have shorter joints than those of the Tiffany eagle; (3) Zeitler cut fewer distinguished barbs on the butt ends of the arrows; (4) the shape of the letters used for the motto "E Pluribus unum" was modified.

IMPRESSION FROM THE DIE OF 1904

OBVERSE

REVERSE

35

The lawful design of the Great Seal of the United States, finally accepted by Congress (in use today), consists of three separate parts. In the order of their importance, they are as follows: The Arms, The Crest, and The Reverse. Both the Arms and Crest are found upon the Obverse face of the Seal; the Reverse stands alone and counterbalances the rest. Strictly speaking, the Reverse is the "counter-sigillum" (counter-seal) of the Arms alone, and the Crest is an independent device. Upon the Seal, however, it is naturally placed over the Arms, and at the middle chief-point of the Obverse.

Although Congress had appropriated the funds (in 1884) for the "obverse and reverse of the seal of the United States," the Reverse Seal was not cut. Five times the "acts of Congress" relating to the Reverse Seal were ignored (1782, 1789, 1833, 1884 and 1902). Finally, in 1935, exactly 153 years after its adoption, a die was cut and has since been a decoration on the back of one dollar bills. Henry A. Wallace (former Vice-President) has taken credit for making the suggestion which eventually led to the inclusion of the Reverse Seal on the dollar bill. Wallace later recorded the sequence of events as follows:

"In 1934, when I was Secretary of Agriculture, I was waiting in the outer office of Secretary Hull, and as I waited I amused myself by picking up a State Department publication which was on a stand there entitled, *The History of the Seal of the United States.* Turning to page 53, I noted the colored reproduction of the reverse side of the Seal. The Latin phrase Novus Ordo Seclorum impressed me as meaning the New Deal of the Ages. Therefore I took the publication to President Roosevelt and suggested a coin be put out with the obverse and reverse sides of the Seal. Roosevelt, as he looked at [the] colored reproduction of the Seal, was first struck with the representation of the 'All-Seeing Eye,' a representation of The Great Architect of the Universe. Next he was impressed with the idea that the foundation for the new order of the ages had been laid in 1776, but that it would be completed only under the eye of the Great Architect. Roosevelt, like myself, was a 32nd degree Mason. He suggested that the Seal be put out on the dollar bill rather than a coin, and took the matter up with the Secretary of the Treasury. When the first draft came back from the Treasury, the obverse side was on the left of the bill as is heraldic practice. Roosevelt insisted that the order be reversed so that the phrase 'of the United States' would be under the obverse side of the Seal. I believe he was also responsible for introducing the word 'Great' in the phrase 'The Great Seal' as it is found under the reverse side of the Seal on the left of our dollar bills. Roosevelt was a great stickler for details and loved playing with them, no matter whether it involved the architecture of a house, a post office or a dollar bill."

MODEL OF THE BACK OF THE DOLLAR BILL (SERIES 1935), WITH PRESIDENT ROOSEVELT'S ANNOTATIONS

THE ARMS

The National Arms displays, as its central figure, the American Bald Eagle with a shield of 13 red and white paleways banded across the top with a blue chief (band). From the eagle's beak flutters a scroll bearing, in 13 letters, the motto, "E. Pluribus Unum." In the eagle's right talon is an olive branch with 13 leaves and 13 berries. In its left talon is carried 13 arrows fledged with 13 feathers.

The devices making up our National Arms are in the order of their importance as follows: 1. The Eagle, 2. The Escutcheon, 3. The Scroll, 4. The Motto, 5. The Olive-branch, 6. The Bundle of Arrows. We shall examine these six heraldic elements separately.

1. THE EAGLE

The American Bald Eagle or white-headed eagle is the strongest and most courageous member of the Aquila (Leucocephalus) family of Falcons. Full grown, its height is about three feet. It is of a glossy brown-ash color with head and tail white, iris white, over which is a prominence covered with yellow skin; its beak and cere are a deep yellow, as are the legs and feet; its talons are black. Nature has endowed the Bald Eagle with great strength and powerful wings, extending seven feet, more or less. The eagle (in heraldry) is accounted one of the most noble figures in armoury, and according to authorities in this science "ought to be given to none but such that greatly excel in the virtues of generosity and courage . . ." (C.A.L. Totten) The eagle on metals (and so on dies) is a symbol of Divinity and Providence. It was also an ancient symbol of spiritual vision.

In American heraldry, the Eagle symbolizes the "People of the United States," who, speaking with sovereign voice in the Preamble to their Constitution, expressly show themselves to constitute the government with power inherent in themselves alone to "ordain and establish" its form. (Preamble: "We the People of the

United States, in order to form a more perfect union, establish justice, insure domestic tranquility, provide for the common defense, promote the general welfare, and secure the blessings of liberty to ourselves and our posterity, do ordain and establish this Constitution for the United States of America.")

The Eagle first appeared in American heraldry upon the flag of Washington's Life Guard, with the shield upon its breast. It was employed by William Barton in one of his early designs for the Seal. It owes its central prominence, upon the Arms, to Secretary Thomson's genius in associating all the best elements into one harmonious whole, whose heraldic accuracy was finally completed by Barton.

In Scripture, the Eagle is declared one of the loftiest emblems of nationality (Ezek. 17:3-7). Deut. 28:49 refers to its swiftness. According to Audubon (the American naturalist), the eagle can sail along with broad extended wings and then ascend until it disappears from view without any apparent motion. Then from the greatest height, it can descend upon its quarry with a rapidity which cannot be followed by the eye.

Job 39:29 refers to the eagle's piercing eye. The eagle has a little eye but a very quick sight to discern its prey afar off. It is also supposed to be the only creature that can look directly into the sun. Job 39:30 refers to the eagle's courage. Although formidable to all birds, the eagle does not prey on small birds, and often leaves a part of its kill for other birds that follow. However, it does not permit other birds of prey to gain a

tenure in the vicinity of its eyrie (nest). Thus it has its own peculiar doctrine against foreign encroachment, and is unrelenting in its strict enforcement. (Compare this with the principles of the "Monroe Doctrine.")

Eagles usually mate once and build one eyrie that serves them for the remainder of their lives. Their eyries are built most frequently on some flat surface upon the highest and most precipitous rocks. (See Job 39:28.) It is with remarkable solicitude that the eagle protects the young eaglets and teaches them to fly. In doing so, if the young birds become weary or fearful, it takes them upon its back and carries them to safety. In allusion to this most beautiful trait we have the story of how God delivered His people out of Egypt and bore them upon "eagles' wings" (Exod. 19:4).

Revelation 12:14 tells of the "woman" (Israel) fleeing into the wilderness and being given *"two wings of a great eagle."* Thus we find the eagle is a glowing emblem of Divine Providence that in so many instances prospered our undertakings. This unrivaled King of the Air is a worthy representative of the genius of American liberty. Self-reliant, the eagle in heraldry needs no supporters and is most fittingly given the chief place upon our "Coat of Arms."

2. THE ESCUTCHEON

In heraldry there can be no coat of arms without a shield. It is the shield upon the existence of which everything else hangs or depends, and it is the shield which is of first and greatest importance. The shield or Escutcheon of the Great Seal carries 13 paleways, banded across the top in blue. Each stripe is of equal width – seven of them white and six red. The official explanation of the shield's symbolism is that the red and white stripes represent the original 13 colonies – supported by the blue chief which unites the whole and represents Congress. Barton explains: "The pales in the arms are kept closely united by the chief, and the latter depends on that union, and the strength resulting from it, for its support, to denote the Confederacy of the United States, and the preservation of their union through Congress . . . The Escutcheon is borne on the breast of an American Eagle, without any other Supporter, to denote that the United States of America ought to rely on their own virtue."

The colors of the paleways on the Escutcheon are taken from the American Flag – White, signifying "Purity and Innocence," and Red, signifying "Vigilance, Perseverance and Justice." It is to be noted that the colors as used on the Escutcheon are reverse from the order of the Flag, which begins in Red and ends in Red, showing an incompleted task. The Escutcheon begins in White and ends in White, showing a task completed. In symbolism, the Flag portrays national interests, while the Escutcheon portrays spiritual interests.

The scriptural significance of the colors used on the Escutcheon are: Red, the color of blood, signifies "Justice" or "Judgement," reminding us of the blood of Christ shed for us. White, the color of snow, signifies "Purity" or "Holiness." Blue, the color of the sky, signifies "Love." Because this is the color of the heavens, it is also representative of God. Blue is also given as a remembrance of Law (Num. 15:38,39).

From earliest times the shield has been the most honored of defensive arms. In modern times, though its distinctive use has all but passed away, its deep significance has continued to remain among all peoples as the emblem of supreme protection. The Scriptures give glowing similes to shields withdrawn: ". . . *who is like unto thee O people saved by the Lord, the shield of thy help*"; (Deut. 33:29) "*Fear not, Abram: I am thy shield, and thy exceeding great reward*"; (Gen. 15:1) "*For thou, Lord, wilt bless the righteous; with favour wilt thou compass him as with a shield*"; (Psalm 5:12) "*He shall cover thee with his feathers and under his wings shalt thou trust: his truth shall be thy shield and buckler.*" (Psalm 91:4)

The Escutcheon of America is her glorious "Constitution," but in a spiritual sense symbolizes the "Shield of Faith," which protects our nation from the evil designs of our enemies: *"Above all, taking the shield of faith, wherewith ye shall be able to quench all of the fiery darts of the wicked."* (Eph. 6:16) It is this "Shield" only, in a symbolical sense, that the self reliant Eagle needs to guard its offspring.

3. THE SCROLL

The placing of the Scroll in the beak of the Eagle was Secretary Thomson's idea. This arrangement is not only unique but solitary in national heraldry. Generally they are placed either below the Escutcheon, or over the Crest. Although the Statute makes no mention of its color, in the official blazonry of the State Department its tincture is gold, and the motto is lettered thereon in a nondescript neutral tint.

Scrolls were originally the books of the ancients, and in heraldry this device is the emblem of a "Book." In former times all books were written upon rolls of linen papyrus, parchment, or prepared lamb's skins. In latter days, when heraldry selected its symbols, the whole record of life was supposed to be worthily transcribed, when on his Scroll a knight wrote his motto only. Often they were rolled up for better preservation, and frequently, where of great import, as in prophetic writings, they were sealed and stored in cases. From this practice of rolling scrolls is derived the word "volum," from the

Latin word "volvere," meaning "to roll." The Scroll borne by the American Eagle is an unsealed one, rolled out, and its sentiments openly displayed.

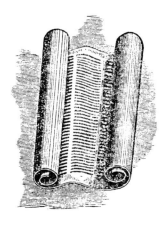

4. THE MOTTO – E. PLURIBUS UNUM

Mottoes in heraldry had their origin in the war cries of knights. They were also honorably borne in times of peace, and their sentiment was made a rule of life. So the National Motto of the Great American People, "E. Pluribus Unum," borne in the beak of the Eagle, is its war cry as well as its lofty guide to higher life.

Our now famous Motto was first proposed by Thomas Jefferson and was formally adopted by the committee of 1776. Inspiration for the Motto may have been the Continental Silver Dollar and the design upon one of the Colonial Bills then in circulation. Both carried the words, "We are One," more appropriately designed "One Out of Many" (made or constructed out of many). This gives National testimony to the fact that as a nation we sprang out from many nations or tribes.

The theme of our National Motto can readily be seen in several noted passages in the Bible, where almost the exact phraseology is employed. One of them is particularly remarkable, not only for its use of the expression, but from its Anglo-Israelite sentiments. It refers to the stars of heaven so beautifully chosen for our Crest. It occurs in the Epistle of Paul to the Hebrews from which we extract the following: *"By faith Abraham, when he was called to go out into a place which he should after receive for an inheritance, obeyed; and he went out, not knowing whither he went . . . Through faith also Sara herself received strength to conceive seed, and was delivered of a child when she was past age, because she judged him faithful who had promised . . . Therefore sprang there even of one, and in him as good as dead, so many as the stars of the sky in multitude, and as the sand which is by the sea shore innumerable . . . By faith, Jacob, when he was dying, blessed both the sons of Joseph."* (Heb. 11:8,11,12,21)

In the above passages, St. Paul informs us from whom "the many," who form his posterity (Abraham, the "one" and father of the faithful), are all descended. To make the reference clearer, he brings Ephraim and Manasseh into the promise by a special mention. This is even clearer when the Lord appeared unto Jacob the second time at Bethel, blessing him and changing his name to "Israel": *"And God said unto him, I am God Almighty: be fruitful and multiply; a nation and a company of nations shall be of thee, and kings shall come out of thy loins."* (Gen. 35:11)

Later, in the land of Egypt, the dying patriarch, Israel, blessed the sons of Joseph, transmitting intact to them, though they were merely children by adoption (his own sons Simeon and Reuben lost their birthright), the whole of the glorious promise: *"The Angel which redeemed me from all evil, bless the lads; and let my name be named on them, and the name of my fathers Abraham and Isaac; and let them grow into a multitude in the midst of the earth.*" (Gen. 48:19) Jacob went on to prophetically bless the children of Manasseh, that they should become the one "great" people, and the children of Ephraim, the "multitude of nations." (Gen. 48:19)

5. THE OLIVE BRANCH

The Olive Branch held in the Eagle's dexter (right) talon consists of 13 leaves and 13 berries, and the official explanation is that it signifies peace. This is taken from the Scriptures where the dove sent out by Noah returned with an olive leaf in its beak (Gen. 8:11). The Statute is not quite explicit in regards to the arrangement of leaves and fruit; only stating it to be "all proper." However, a letter from Tiffany & Co. shows there was a definite intention in the number of leaves and berries. The letter reads:

"We have used the classical olive and decided not to introduce the flowers; the fruit (13) and the 13 leaves speak for themselves in a very clear and positive manner, but the flowers, while they suggest a growing and fruitful future, would, as no special number could be used, give an uncertainty not desirable, as it would always be supposed that the particular number of flowers used must have a meaning while that meaning is not there."

This shows that in making the final designs for the Obverse Seal, great care was taken to introduce nothing not truly significant. Another letter from Tiffany & Co. confirms this view, for it reads: "Mr. James H. Whitehouse was for many years prior to 1900 the chief designer

OLEA EUROPOEA

of our House, and the details of the present seal were perfected and carefully drawn under his personal direction . . . The original details of the design were arranged and decided in 1782."

In the Scriptures, the olive tree is one of the earliest and most sacred symbols of Nationality (Jer. 11:16). Israel is likened unto an "olive tree" (Rom. 11:1-36), its fruit that of "fatness" (Judges 9:9). Jeremiah speaks of the ten-tribed kingdom of Israel, after they were cast out of the land for sin and before they had found grace in the wilderness, in these words: *"The Lord called thy name, A green olive tree, fair, and of goodly fruit . . ."* (Jer. 11:16)

Hosea speaks of the Joseph-Israelitish nation: *"I will be as the dew unto Israel: he shall grow as the lily, and cast forth his roots as Lebanon. His branches shall spread, and his beauty shall be as the olive tree, and his smell as Lebanon."* (Hosea 14:5-6) This prophetic blessing, *"branches shall spread,"* is a continuation of Jacob's blessing of Joseph, which reads: *"Joseph is a fruitful bough, even a fruitful bough by a well; whose branches run over the wall."* (Gen. 49:22) The founding of America is the fulfillment of this promise. Our people landed on these shores as *"branches running over a wall,"* as they were guided and led by Divine Providence.

The Olive Branch is particularly the heraldic device of the tribe of Manasseh (see *Shimeall's Chronology Historic and Prophetic*), and in the whole of the Botanic kingdom, no other plant could have been used more appropriately for recognition as our National Plant as the olive branch. Its place on our National Arms illustrates the Divine command given to the Israelites, as we find in the Book of Deuteronomy: *"When thou comest nigh unto a city to fight against it, then proclaim peace unto it . . . And if it will make no peace with thee, but will make war against thee, then thou shalt besiege it.*" (Deut. 20:10,12) In strict accordance with this Divine precept, America made overtures of peace to our mother country previous to the commencement of the War for Independence (Revolutionary).

6. THE BUNDLE OF ARROWS

The Bundle of Arrows in the Eagle's sinister (left) talon consists of 13 arrows fledged with 13 feathers, and was first proposed by Secretary Thomson. As in the case of the Olive Branch, the Statute is not specific as to details. No mention is made as to color or the direction the Arrows should point. Since the Statute only states, "all proper," they have universally been represented on the Arms with "points upward" and outward. This is their "proper" mode of display as (on the Seal) they represent the war power of the country, which is thus shown to be in a state of readiness and preparation.

The Arrows are most appropriately given the secondary or sinister place in the grasp of the Eagle's talon. America prefers peace to war. We offer first the right hand of friendship. However, we are prepared for conflict: self reliant, possessed of inexhaustible resources and confident in Him who "prospered our beginnings." But Arrows are more than emblems of the power of war. They are symbols of "aim" denoting purpose, will and intention. By combining these ideas with those of the Olive Branch, we may read the symbolism of the Arrows as meaning that it is the cardinal principle of true Americanism that recourse to arms shall be for no other purpose than the maintenance of a just cause having for its object the establishment and preservation of unity and love.

Arrows are also intimately connected with our own traditions as Anglo-Saxon people. The English archers were most feared in every battlefield of the Middle Ages. It was their distinctive weapon, whose flight in deadly clouds decimated the ranks of their adversaries. The Saxon archers could deliver their arrows with such force as to penetrate a two-inch oak board at a distance of over 200 yards.

Further back in history, the bow and arrow was Israel's weapon. The little tribe of Benjamin alone had an army of 280,000 men of valor that *"bare shields and drew the bow."* (II Chron. 14:8) These men possessed such skill that they could use alike *"both the right hand and the left in hurling stones and shooting arrows out of a bow . . ."* (I Chron. 12:2) In his blessing of Joseph, Jacob expressly says that, *"The archers have sorely grieved him, and shot at him, and hated him: But his bow abode in strength, and the arms of his hands were made strong by the hands of the mighty God of Jacob . . ."* (Gen. 49:23,24)

Manasseh, as well as his father Joseph, was well versed in this method of warfare, for we read that *"The sons of Reuben, and the Gadites and half of the tribe of Manasseh, of valiant men, men able to bear buckler and sword, and to shoot with bow, and skillful in war, were four and forty thousand seven hundred and threescore, that went out to the war."* (I Chron. 5:18)

In scriptural symbolism, the Bundle of Arrows represent the weapon of the Almighty. It is the wounding, convicting of sin, "Arrow of the Word," described by the Psalmist: *"Thine arrows stick fast in me, and thy hand presseth me sore."* (Psalm 38:2) This same arrow is the celestial arrow of Sagitta (minor constellation of Capricornus) seen having left the bow and speeding to its aim, and He who shoots it is invisible.

 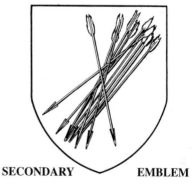

PRIMARY EMBLEM SECONDARY EMBLEM

THE TRIBE OF MANASSEH

THE CREST

In heraldry, the Crest was an ornament for the head. It was usually fastened to the helmet and was a distinctively personal or hereditary device. Warriors among the classical ancients bore insignia peculiar to themselves in this manner. Our National Crest, however, represents America, like a new Constellation, taking its place on high with its light dispelling the clouds and darkness round about its ever expanding limits.

The Crest is composed of three essential parts. These are, in the order enumerated by the Statute, as follows: 1. "The Glory," 2. "The Cloud," 3. "The Constellation." Each of these elements depicts self reliance as does the Arms below the Crest. The Glory, the Cloud and the Stars in nature need no supporters. On our National Crest they float above the Eagle with no need of resting upon any wreath or crown of maintenance. We shall consider each component separately:

1. THE GLORY

The primary significance of a "glory" is to denote the presence of God (Psalm 63:2). It is directly from Scripture that heraldry has borrowed this resplendent symbol of self-radiance: ". . . *and the Glory of the Lord shone round about them.*" (Luke 2:9) This same Glory, in the form of a pillar of Fire at night, gave evidence to the Children of Israel in the Wilderness that the presence of Yahvey was with them: "*And the Lord went before them . . . to lead them the way; and by night in a pillar of fire to give them light; . . .*" (Exodus 13:21) In choosing the Glory as part of our National Crest, we have denoted the presence of the Lord, over and in the midst of our Nation.

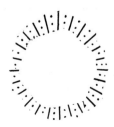

The Statute is silent as to the tincture of the "Glory." Because its designation is "proper," it has been universally accepted as "Gold." Its arrangement, although approved by Congress, has, however, been criticized as a misconception of the Statute which plainly reads: ". . . a glory or, breaking through a cloud." The Cloud should surround the Stars, but the Glory breaking through it should surround the Cloud spreading its rays downward and into the field beyond. In practice, every die cut of the Seal has represented the Glory as surrounded by the Cloud, through which not a single ray has been allowed to break. This violation is not found upon our coinage or the Great Seal Metal.

OBVERSE   **REVERSE**

THE GREAT SEAL CENTENNIAL METAL, 1882

Julia Ward Howe sang of this "Glory" in the inspiring "Battle Hymn of the Republic," in the following words: "Mine eyes have seen the Glory of the Coming of the Lord." She, like the founders of our Republic, envisioned the future establishment of the Kingdom of Heaven on earth. She voiced this vision in the last stanza of her hymn, which is generally never sung and is almost unknown:

"He is coming like the Glory of the morning on the wave,
 He is wisdom to the mighty, He is succor to the brave,
 So the world shall be His footstool and the soul of time His slave,"

2. THE CLOUD

The Cloud which surrounds the Constellation in American heraldry is to be represented, according to the Statute, as "proper." It is therefore designed to be blazoned sable with its inner linings lightened (argent) and illuminated (in roseate and sunset hues – "gules, purpure," etc.) by the effulgence of the stars that it surrounds. The Cloud is represented as rolling back, that other stars may be in time revealed and added to that group.

In symbolism, the Cloud in rolling back indicates the breaking up of the storm of ignorance, injustice and oppression before the dawning light of a new and potent constellation. But, this emblem has deeper significance – that of covering and protecting. The Lord "*sealeth up the stars*," explains Job – using the Hebrew idiom – "*With clouds he covereth the light; and commandeth it not to shine by the cloud that cometh betwixt.*" (Job 36:32) "*He spread a cloud for a covering:*" (Psalm 105:39) This same idea of "protecting" is expressed by Moses just before taking leave of the chosen people.

In Scripture and in nature, the clouds also denote the presence of Yahvey: "*And it came to pass, when the congregation was gathered against Moses and against Aaron, that they looked toward the tabernacle of the congregation: and, behold, the cloud covered it, and the glory of the Lord appeared.*" (Num. 16:42) A cloud guided those that had just escaped from bondage: "*And the Lord went before them by day in a pillar of a cloud, to lead them the way . . .*" (Exod. 13:21)

It was a cloud that stood between the Israelites and the Egyptians: "*And it came between the camp of the Egyptians and the camp of Israel; and it was a cloud and darkness to them, but it gave light by night to these: so that the one came not near the other all the night.*" (Exod. 14:20) The motions of a cloud directed their wanderings and their camps: "*And when the cloud was taken up from the tabernacle, then after that the children of Israel journeyed: and in the place where the cloud abode, there the children of Israel pitched their tents."* (Num. 9:17)

Upon special occasions, the Cloud, generally thick and impenetrable by day, was broken by the Glory of God appearing in it: *"And it came to pass, as Aaron spake unto the whole congregation of the children of Israel, that they looked toward the wilderness, and, behold, the glory of the Lord appeared in the cloud."* (Exod. 16:10)

3. THE CONSTELLATION

The Constellation of 13 stars in the midst of the glory Cloud is composed of pentagrams, or five-pointed stars, so arranged that their groupings form a hexagram, or six-pointed star. This hexagram is composed of two equilateral triangles and in each triangle are exactly ten stars. The Statute is silent as to the arrangement of the stars. For this reason, Professor Totten suggests that in order for the arrangement of the stars in the Crest to be heraldically correct it should be "proper" (according to nature and not in any way confined to the regularity of a circle or to a regular distribution).

A natural arrangement of the stars (in the Constellation) was evidently in the minds of the Committees of 1779 and 1780, as evidenced by the designs they submitted. Charles Thomson's original design also shows a natural arrangement of the stars. Notwithstanding, the final version approved by Congress for our National Seal has the Constellation arranged in the form of a six-pointed star. This arrangement seems to have been fixed and warranted by the earlier seal of the President of the Continental Congress, and may be accounted for by the possibility of the same artist having cut both seals.

It will be noted that the stars of the Constellation were originally designed as six-pointed. As such, Professor Totten points out, "their aggregation into a six-pointed constellation was not incongruous, but as soon as the stars upon the Crest received their true heraldic shape (from adjustment to the Flag) it became so, and the pentalphate form was a natural corollary to the improved conception."

The American, radiant, five-pointed, silver star is believed to have constituted the seal or signet of King Solomon (circ. 1000 B.C.), and in early times it was in use among the Hebrew people as a symbol of safety. In scriptural heraldry we are taught that such a star (five-pointed) was a most ancient way of hieroglyphically representing "Divine Providence."

The Constellation of 13 stars was meant particularly to symbolize this nation formed of 13 independent States. However, in scriptural symbolism, they also represent the 13 tribes of Israel. This is shown in the prophetic dream of Joseph in which we find the 13 heavenly bodies: the 11 stars, the sun and the moon, making abeisance to him. The interpretation given in the Scriptures is that the 11 stars represent the 11 other sons of Jacob, or tribes of Israel (Gen. 37:5-11).

Joseph, the one receiving the homage, later gave up his tribalship in favor of his two sons, Ephraim and Manasseh. Jacob, in adopting the two sons, placed the younger son, Ephraim, ahead of Manasseh. Consequently, Ephraim took Joseph's place (the 11th tribe), leaving Manasseh, who came after Benjamin, to become the 13th tribe.

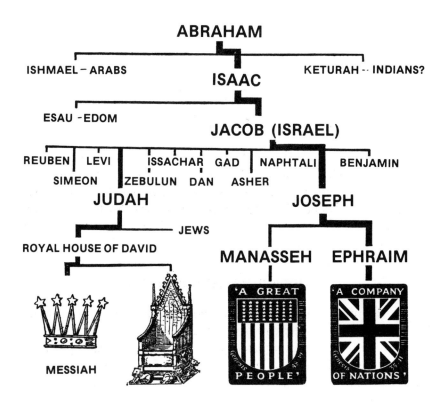

Levi was removed from being numbered among the tribes, so the Bible continues to speak of the "12 tribes of Israel."

Ephraim and Manasseh, together, form the two branches of the tribe of Joseph and are the recipients of Jacob's blessing of Joseph: *"His glory is like the firstling of his bullock, and his horns are like the horns of unicorns: with them he shall push the people together to the ends of the earth: and they are the ten thousands of Ephraim, and they are the thousands of Manasseh."* (Deut. 33:17)

THE REVERSE SEAL

The true object of a reverse seal is to guard against its falsification. In former times, to accomplish this, a "counter-seal" was used. The custody of the two seals was then given to different guardians. Usually, the reverse seal was used only on documents of the highest importance. Today, the Statute gives the custody of the entire Seal (Reverse as well as Obverse) into the hands of the same individual, the Secretary of State.

The Reverse face of the Great Seal consists of six essential elements: 1. "The Unfinished Pyramid," 2. "The Mystical Eye," 3. "The Radiant Triangle" (constituting the "Reverse Crest"), 4. The words "Annuit Coeptis," 5. The motto "Novus Ordo Seclorum," 6. The numerical letters "MDCCLXXVI." We shall examine each element separately.

1. THE UNFINISHED PYRAMID

The unfinished Pyramid is the most prominent device on the Reverse Seal; the counterpart, so-to-speak, of the Arms (Obverse). It is composed of 13 courses of masonry. The official explanation is that it represents the Great Pyramid of Giza, in Egypt, and symbolizes "strength" and "duration."

The Great Pyramid of Giza is the most gigantic building ever erected upon the face of the earth. It is over 4500 years old and still a masterpiece of architecture. Built of stone and literally founded both in and on the rock, it is preeminently the emblem of lasting stability. Students of the Pyramid have come to the conclusion that it is the "pillar" to which Isaiah 19:19 refers: *"In that day there shall be an altar to the Lord in the midst of the land of Egypt, and a pillar* [monument] *at the border thereof to the Lord."*

The seemingly mathematical impossibility of the monument of Isaiah being located at the center and the border of the land of Egypt at the same time was solved by the great American geographer, Henry Michell (chief hydographer to the United States Coast Survey – 1868). Michell discovered that the Great Pyramid was mathematically located at the center of the circular section forming Lower Egypt or the Delta of the Nile. It was thus at once upon the center and the border of Lower Egypt and Upper Egypt. Occupying the central point of the mutual and central borders of both Egypts, the Pyramid therefore stands at the center of all Egypt. The location thus fits Isaiah's description and establishes the structure *"for a sign and for a witness to the Lord of Hosts."* (Isaiah 19:20)

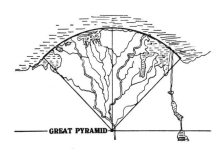

GREAT PYRAMID

The study of the Great Pyramid over the past one hundred years has established its claim to being that monument beyond all doubt. It is our privilege and our duty to re-explore this structure and to unravel its teachings and recognize its relevance to America and its people. (For a condensed resume of the subject, the reader is referred to *The Great Pyramid Decoded* – Capt – listed on inside rear cover.)

It is significant that the Unfinished Great Pyramid was one of the great national monuments of the country where Joseph married and his two sons, Ephraim and Manasseh were born. The Great Pyramid was also a reminder of the Children of Israel's long sojourn in the land of Egypt. Again we find, as with many other aspects of the Great Seal, Israelitish origins.

2. THE MYSTICAL EYE

The "Eye of Providence" was first proposed by Du Simitiere, and the conception of surrounding it with the "Radiant Triangle" was Thomas Jefferson's suggestion. Both Barton and Thomson retained the idea and Congress adopted it. The Statute of June 20th, 1782, reads as follows: "In the Zenith an Eye in a Triangle surrounded with a Glory, proper:" The tincture of the Glory is, of course, "Or" (gold) but the "proper" heraldic blazonry of the All-seeing Eye is not clearly defined. Since the "Eye," is an emblem of God, Himself, who can assign a special "color" to the Eye of the Omniscient? Totten suggests: "This symbol can be blazoned 'properly' only as of argent (white). The laws of Correspondence, Heraldry and Harmony all conspire in this selection. White, ineffable, clear as the firmament above . . . heraldry that dares not stain such an emblem with any arbitrary color (white is not a color but is every color combined) . . ."

The emblem of the "Eye" is one of the most ancient symbols of "Divine Providence," and is found among the earliest nations of the earth. The Greeks swore by the "Eye of Jove," and his worship spread over the Roman world. The "Solar Eye," as it was known, became a religious badge in all the ancient world. But the device has an older origin. It was the symbol of the Arabian god of Jethro (the father-in-law of Moses), and was a resplendent sun inscribed with the Arabic motto, "Allah" or "I am that I am." The earliest use of the "Eye of Providence" appears to have been in ancient Chaldea, the early homeland of the Hebrew people.

In our American heraldry, the Eye symbolizes the watchful God of Israel watching over the destiny of this nation and illustrating the prophetic words: *"Behold, he that keepeth Israel shall neither slumber nor sleep."* (Psa. 121:4) Concerning Israel, the Lord has said, *"I will set mine eyes upon them for good . . ."* (Jer. 24:6) In Psalm 32:8, God promises Israel: *". . . I will guide thee with mine eye."* In the Book of Deuteronomy we find this reference to ·the "Divine Eye" with Israel: *"He found him in a desert land, and in the waste howling wilderness: He led him about, he instructed him, he kept him as the apple of his eye."* (Deut. 32:10)

3. THE RADIANT TRIANGLE

The mystical triangle that encases the Eye is also an emblem of great antiquity. The solar triangle of the Egyptians was a symbol of Osiris, Isis, and Orus, and was inscribed with the mystic motto, "I am all that was, that is and that shall be." Among the aboriginal coins of America (described in Dickerson's *Numismatic Manual*), there is a very interesting one of terra cotta bearing the exact representation of the mysterious triangle.

Allusion to this triangle is found in most of the ancient religious and secret societies. Ancient Freemasonry employed the triangle, generally in connection with the All-Seeing Eye. Throughout the whole system of modern Masonry, there is no symbol more important in its significance, or more various in its application, than the triangle. It is held in the highest esteem by all Royal Arch Masons, whose Altar is triangular, whose Jewels are triangular, etc. The triangle, in connection with the All-Seeing Eye, is the Masonic symbol of the "Grand Architect of the Universe."

In heraldry, when a triangle is placed within and surrounded by a circle of rays, the circle is called a "Glory" (Christian). When, however, this Glory is distinct from the triangle (as in the case of the Reverse Seal) it is then an emblem of "God's Eternal Glory." This is the usual form in religious uses.

The Radiant Triangle making up part of the Crest of the Reverse Seal forms the Cap-Stone or "Corner Stone" of the Unfinished Pyramid. In the Scriptures, Jesus Christ is symbolized by just such a "stone": *"The stone which the builders rejected, the same is become the head of the corner: this is the Lord's doing, and it is marvelous in our eyes."* (Matthew 21:42 quoted from Psalm 118:22,23) And, *". . . Jesus Christ himself being the chief corner stone; In whom all the building fitly framed together groweth unto an holy temple in the Lord."* (Eph. 2:20,21)

4. THE MOTTO – ANNUIT COEPTIS

Above the Reverse Crest, in 13 letters, is the motto, "Annuit Coeptis," meaning "He hath prospered our undertakings" (or beginnings). These beautiful sentiments upon the Seal refer directly to the "All-Seeing Eye" in the "Radiant Triangle," as an emblem of Him who prospered our undertakings. In a secondary sense, it refers to the Unfinished Pyramid below, whose 13 courses of stone grow up in lasting stability toward the Cap-stone descending from the Sky.

Barton's earlier and more complicated design contained the motto "Deo Favente" (with God's favor) placed over the Eye. Although it meant essentially the same thing, Secretary Thomson changed to the present and even more deeply significant motto, "Annuit Coeptis." Although it may have been suggested in total blindness to its mystic Anglo-Israelite significance, the change displays more clearly America's Israel birthright.

The fact that the present motto possesses 13 letters adds intensity to this important reference. Its hidden meaning has reference primarily to the children of Manasseh. As the 13th tribe of Israel, they were particularly set apart to have their undertakings prospered as a separate people, whose greatness in the latter times was prophetically assured.

The birthright of temporal blessings was but a continuation of the prosperity promised Manasseh's father, Joseph: *"And the Lord was with Joseph, and he was a prosperous man"*; and *"the Lord made all that he did to prosper in his hand."* (Gen. 39:2,3) *"And of Joseph he said, Blessed of the Lord be his land, for the precious things of heaven, for the dew, and for the deep that coucheth beneath, and for the precious fruits brought forth by the sun, and for the precious things put forth by the moon. And for the chief things of the ancient mountains, and for the precious things of the lasting hills."* (Deut. 33:13-15)

5. THE MOTTO – NOVUS ORDO SECLORUM

The motto, "Novus Ordo Seclorum," written in Latin words is an intentionally altered quotation from Virgil's *Fourth Eclogue*. It was borrowed, in turn, by Virgil from the mystic Sibylline records (The Sibylline Books). These books were a collection of prophetic writings; one is supposed to contain the fate of the Roman Empire. The original books date back to around 1000 B.C. Copies are believed to have been in existence as late as the fourth century A.D. and destroyed by the Emperor Honorus. The books derive their name from "Sibylla," a female Daniel of those early days who became a mythical figure. The

Encyclopaedia Britannica states that the Sibylline Books were of Semitic origin, written at a time when prophets abounded in Greece and Asia Minor.

It was from these ancient Hebrew prophecies and heroes of early Israel that the fascinating mythology of ancient Greece was derived. But they were colored so fantastically that they were considered by the scholars to be only pagan myths. Few scholars are aware that the Greek Hercules is the biblical Samson. The Roman god Saturn is the Greek god Krones, and the latter was the Greek name for Israel or Jacob (according to the Phoenician writer Sanchoniathon, who was contemporary of Homer).

Although many Jewish forgeries have appeared from time to time, fragments of the Sibylline writings, believed to be of the original writings, contain many remarkable prophecies that have certainly met with accurate fulfillment. Some of them seemed to have looked forward to our own times and country.

Virgil wrote:

"Ultima Cumaei venit jam carminis aetas;
Magnus ab intergro saeclorum nascitur ordo.
Jam redit et Virgo, redeunt Saturnia regna;
Jam nova progenies caelo demittitur alto;
Tu modo nascenti puero, quo ferrea primun
Desinet ac toto surget gens aurea mundo,
Casta, fave, Lucina, . . ."

"The last age of Cumean song now comes.
Novus ordo seclorum – a mighty Order of Ages is born Anew.
Both the prophetic Virgin, and the Saturnian kingdoms now return.
Now a new progeny is let down from the lofty heavens.
Favor, chaste Lucina, the boy soon to be born.
In whom the Iron age shall come to end.
And the Golden one rise again in the whole earth ..."

Translation application to America:

"The last age of Cumean song now comes (the seventh or last, or perfect cycle).

Novus ordo seclorum (the Sabbatic age of Rest – the Age of Freedom) a mighty Order of Ages is born Anew.

Both the Prophetic Virgin (Goddess of Liberty) and the Saturnian kingdoms (the new Republic – Kingdom of Israel) now return (in the latter days).

Now a new progeny (a progeny among nations, diverse from all predecessors – a government "of the people, by the people, and for the people": – a nation of independent States, and yet the union of a multitude of individuals) is let down from the lofty heavens (the sign of Divine Providence in our behalf).

Favor, chaste Lucina, the boy (young America) soon to be born.

In whom the Iron age (Old World ideas and bondage) shall come to end.

And the Golden one (individual liberty, freedom and progress) rise again in the whole earth."

It is evident that whatever may have been the reason proposed to himself by the designer of this motto, "Novus Ordo Seclorum," he purposely altered it from the original "magnus saeclorum ordo" in three essential particulars: the "magnus" was changed to "novus"; the spelling of "saeclorum" was altered to the more modern form of "seclorum"; and the order of the words was likewise altered. Nevertheless the derivation of the motto from the Sibylline books through Virgil's *Fourth Eclogue* is clear.

This Sibylline Motto not only harmonizes intimately with the Reverse of the Seal itself but most fittingly complements the symbolism of the Obverse face of the Seal. The Motto also is particularly pointed in its reference to the birth and genius of American institutions that are firmly established, and whose full development no hand can now stay from reaching the final goal of their most perfect realization.

6. THE DATE - MDCCLXXVI

The date MDCCLXXVI (1776) on the base of the Unfinished Pyramid is the date of our Independence. It tells when Divine Providence "prospered our beginnings" (Annuit Coeptis); the beginning of a new nation (Novus Ordo Seclorum) established upon new principles – the nucleus of the Kingdom of God on earth, with all its glorious promises to long-oppressed humanity.

It is most appropriate that the date 1776 is placed upon the base of the symbol of our great national structure that holds the central place upon the Reverse face of the Seal. This date not only marks the beginning of the "New Order of the Ages," but also marks the prophetic date when the children of Manasseh were to be separated from their father's house (Jacob's) to become the "Great People." A.D. 1776 is exactly 7 times (7 X 360 years) or 2520 years from the captivity of the Tribe of Manasseh by the Assyrians in 745 B.C. The "7 times" (2520 years) punishment period was prophesied against each of the tribes of Israel for their sins:

For the Lord shall smite Israel, as a reed is shaken in the water, and he shall root up Israel out of this good land, which he gave to their fathers, and shall scatter them beyond the river [Euphrates], *because they have made their groves, provoking the Lord to anger."* (I Kings 14:15) This prophecy was fulfilled between 745 B.C. and 721 B.C., when all the Northern Kingdom of Israel were carried away by the Assyrians to Media and Northern Mesopotamia. Later, most of the Southern Kingdom of Judah were captured by the Assyrians, under Sennacharib, and united with their fellow Israelites in captivity. There they all became known as the so-called "Lost Tribes of Israel."

The inhabitants of the city of Jerusalem, that had escaped deportation to Assyria, were later captured by Nebuchadnezzar, king of Babylon, and taken to Babylon. In 539 B.C., after Cyrus, king of the Persians, overthrew the Babylonian Empire, he permitted the remnant of Judah in Babylon to return to their homeland. It was this "remnant," together with the Edomites (who had settled in Jerusalem during the Babylonian captivity) and the Babylonians (who returned with the Israelites) that collectively became known as the Nation of the Jews. The name "Jew" (which means "remnant of Judah") had never been applied to any branch of the Semitic peoples prior to the Babylonian captivity, nor can it properly be utilized to designate any of the other "Lost Tribes of Israel." (Failure to recognize this distinction is why there is so much confusion among students of the Bible interpreting the prophetic Scriptures concerning "Israel" or the "Jew.")

The theory (generally held in disrepute) that the Lost Tribes of Israel migrated west from the lands of their captivity to settle in Western Europe, the Isles in the West, and many on to America, the "land in the Wilderness," has in recent years been found by archaeologists to be factual. These amazing findings are based on Assyrian cuneiform tablets identifying the name changes of the Israelites till they became both the "Cimmerians" and the "Scythians." It is common knowledge that the Cimmerians and the Scythians became the Anglo-Saxon, Scandinavian, Germanic, Lombardic, Celtic and kindred peoples. This is the fulfillment of God's promise to Israel: *"Hear the word of the Lord, O ye nations, and declare it in the isles afar off, and say, He that scattered Israel will gather him, and keep him, as a shepherd doth his flock."* (Jer. 31:10)

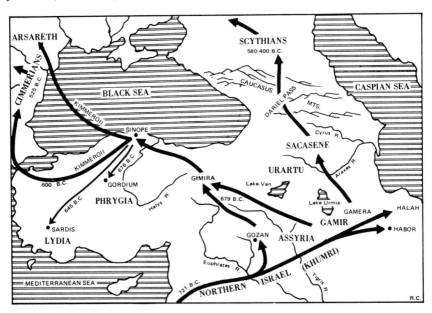

"Lost Israel" being found fulfills yet another Bible prophecy concerning Israel. *"Moreover, I will appoint a place for my people Israel and will plant them, that they may dwell in a place of their own, and move no more, neither shall the children of wickedness afflict them any more, as beforetime."* (II Sam. 7:10) Since the Israelites were then in Palestine, it follows that the "appointed place" had to be somewhere else.

To the Israelites this must have been a strange saying. They had a place – the land of Palestine – and they were established there in peace and power. Nothing seemed less probable than that they should ever move. Yet here was a plain declaration that Israel should be moved to a new place outside of Palestine, from which they should be moved no more.

Another characteristic "mark" whereby Israel could be identified in the latter days is its form of government. *"And their nobles shall be of themselves, and their governor shall proceed from the midst of them."* (Jer. 30:21) What Jeremiah is prophesying is a nation of the people, by the people, and for the people – a nation in which the people are supreme – a Republic. *"And I will restore thy judges as at the first, and thy counsellors as at the beginning: afterward thou shalt be called the city of righteousness, the faithful city."* (Isa. 1:26) Ancient Israel began as a "theocratic" republic. The passage in Isaiah promises that the officers necessary to constitute a republican form of government would be restored, and the elective franchise would be free. The people would possess the sovereign right of choosing their own rulers and judges. The Divine right of kings finds no authority here, for the power invested in the people allows for no monarchy, limited or absolute.

Our Pilgrim Fathers called themselves the "Seed of Abraham," "God's Servants," "Children of Jacob," "His Chosen." They followed after the council of Moses, the lawgiver of Israel, and in all their undertakings asked for guidance and the blessings of the God of Abraham, Isaac and Jacob. The evidence blazoned on the Great Seal is that the founders of this nation came from the tribe of Manasseh. The name, "Manasseh," means "forgetfulness," and if there has ever been a people forgetful of all their past, it is the last, this thirteenth, this Manasseh-Israel people of the United States. However, America, as prophesied of Manasseh, did become the great nation, "E. Pluribus Unum" (One Out of Many), and took her place at the appointed time in fulfillment of God's covenant with Abraham, Isaac, Jacob and Joseph.

PLYMOUTH ROCK

On Monday, December 21, 1620, the Pilgrims from the Mayflower came ashore on "Plymouth Rock," in Cape Cod Bay, Massachusetts to plant their colony. Today, descendants from this original stock are found in all the fifty states of the Union.

THE GREAT SEAL AS A WHOLE

The Great Seal given to our country, after years of laborious heraldic and symbolic study, reveals our true national origin and destiny. The Obverse face is Israel in the Old Testament; the Reverse face, our race under the New Covenant. Each face is a masterful harmony of all that is potent in symbolism and prophecy. It was originated and adopted by men who recognized the overshadowing presence of the Great Architect of the Universe, and the need to submit to His will as revealed in the Scriptures and the Laws of Nature. They planned a government in conformity to His great Plan. They recognized that America's greatest task was to go toward the goal of that Plan – the eventual establishment of the Kingdom of God on earth.

OBVERSE   **REVERSE**

Their hands were guided by another, for seemingly they did not fully know themselves to be of the Tribe of Manasseh. (*"Blindness in part is happened to Israel..."* Rom. 11:25) Yet, wittingly or unwittingly, they used all the national emblems of ancient Israel as America's emblems also. Our Obverse Seal sums up the whole of the Old World history of Israel, whose boundaries were set at the very beginning according to the number of the sons of Jacob, and the Lord as an "Eagle" was his express guardian and "Shield." Unsealed "Truth," borne by the Eagle's beak, illuminated the way of the *"people saved by the Lord."* The blessings and the curses were plainly set before them in the "Olive-Branch" and the "Bundle of Arrows." The "Constellation of Stars" signifies perpetual endurance. The Almighty God himself swore by them as such (Dan. 12:3).

The Reverse Seal is the concentrated emblem of the "New Covenant." It is Israelitish in the first place, founded upon the "Rock" of history itself and in the actual experience of our Race. Hence, when we state that "He prospered our beginnings," we admit our Origin, proclaim our History, and accept our Destiny as Israel. Israel's final state is typified by the Pyramid – a *"building, fitly framed together*

66

groweth unto an holy temple in the Lord: In whom ye also are builded together for an habitation of God through the Spirit." (Eph. 2:21,22)

The "Eye" and the "Radiant Triangle" is the symbol of the Everlasting God of Israel. The significance of the words, "Annuit Coeptis," can be traced directly to the Bible and its numberless and mystic references to the People sealed thereby. July 4th, 1776, ended Manasseh's seven-times punishment and gave birth to the "Novus Ordo Seclorum," itself only a type or prophecy of the Kingdom of God. This Kingdom has yet to be perfected, and it is on this account that we are still in the throes of transition. The day is breaking. The sun of Liberty, whose rising marked the dawn of ages anew in 1776, has now cleared the horizon and ascends to mount the zenith where its perfect light will cover the earth. Then all nations and tongues shall flow to the New Jerusalem to know the Truth which maketh free indeed.

The Great Seal also symbolizes the vision our Forefathers held when they wrote the Declaration of Independence. That they searched the Scriptures is beyond all question. From its pages they found those conceptions of God, Man and Universe which were briefly proclaimed in the Declaration of Independence, more explicitly worked out in the Constitution, and most admirably symbolized by the Great Seal.

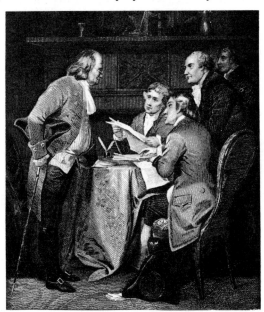

WRITING THE DECLARATION OF INDEPENDENCE
BENJAMIN FRANKLIN   THOMAS JEFFERSON   ROBERT LIVINGSTON
JOHN ADAMS   ROGER SHERMAN

Religion was the dynamics of our nation, and its spiritual influence was evident at the Constitutional Convention in 1787 at Philadelphia. It was Benjamin Franklin's exhortation to prayer that broke the deadlock over Congressional representation. "Gentlemen, I have lived a long time and am convinced that God governs the affairs of men. If a sparrow cannot fall to the ground without His notice, is it probable that an empire can rise without His aid? I, therefore, move that prayers imploring the assistance of Heaven be held every morning before we proceed to business."

Jefferson said in his inaugural address, they were ". . . enlightened by a benign religion, professed indeed and practiced in various forms, yet all of them inculcating honesty, truth, temperance, gratitude, and the love of man, acknowledging and adoring an overruling Providence, which, by all its dispensations, proves that it delights in the happiness of man here, and his greater happiness hereafter."

It is to the honor of Freemasonry that many of the men who framed the Declaration of Independence and served on the various committees to design the Great Seal were members of that fraternity. The pattern of the "New World Order," as shown by the symbolism of the Seal, rests upon the Masonic virtues of "Fortitude," "Prudence," "Temperance" and "Justice." "Fortitude" is represented by hardiness and valour symbolized by the color red. "Temperance" is implied by purity symbolized by white. "Justice and Prudence" are represented by vigilance and perseverance (mentioned in the Act of 1782), symbolized by the color blue.

None of these human virtues can arrive at full fruition without the aid and favor of Divine Providence. No system of government that ignores or denies God can be truly great. No system of economics which does not take Him into account can be in harmony with the great principles to which the Revolutionary heroes pledged their lives, their fortunes and their sacred honor. "Unless we are governed by God, we will be ruled by tyrants," said that great Quaker, William Penn.

It is also the Masonic teachings of liberty, equality and fraternity that became the foundation of Americanism. "Liberty" – the right to life, liberty and property is a God-given right. "Equality" – human equality is equality in the sight of God, and implies that every man may, sooner or later, attain to mastery of self and circumstances. (The equality of man is not equality of ability or capacity.) "Fraternity" – God lives in man, so that every human personality is venerable and holy as the living shrine of the indwelling presence of the Lord: *"Behold, how good and how pleasant it is for brethren to dwell together in unity."* (Psalm 133:1)

AMERICA, THE BEAUTIFUL

O, beautiful for spacious skies,
For amber waves of grain,
For purple mountain majesties
Above the fruited plain!
America! America!
God shed His grace on thee,
And crown thy good with brotherhood
From sea to shining sea!

O, beautiful for pilgrim feet,
Whose stern, impassioned stress
A thoroughfare for freedom beat
Across the wilderness!
America! America!
God mend thine every flaw,
Confirm thy soul in self-control,
Thy liberty in law!

O, beautiful for heroes proved
In liberating strife,
Who more than self their country loved,
And mercy more than life!
America! America!
May God thy gold refine,
'Til all success be nobleness,
And every gain divine!

O, beautiful for patriot dream
That sees beyond the years
Thine alabaster cities gleam
Undimmed by human tears!
America! America!
God shed His grace on thee
And crown thy good with brotherhood
From sea to shining sea!

– Katherine Lee Bates

UNITED STATES IN BIBLE PROPHECY

Whenever God has a place in His providence for a man or a nation we would expect to find such mentioned in Bible prophecy. Rev. F. E. Pitts of Nashville, Tennessee, in his address to the Congress of the United States in 1857 (recorded in the Congressional Records), spoke the following words: "There are very many passages of Scripture which are universally admitted, by the learned and judicious, to foretell the rise of a great nationality in the latter times. These predictions cannot, by any reasonable construction, be applied to the rise of such nationality in the land of Judea; but are most wonderfully descriptive of the United States of America, and of no other country under heaven."

There is a short chapter in Isaiah which means nothing to any commentator, preacher or layman unless he has discovered that the Prophet Isaiah was given a vision of America as existing and playing a conspicuous part in the providence of God among the nations of the earth. The text is in that part of Isaiah where "the burdens" of the various nations are given, or, as the margin states: "The Oracle concerning Babylon which Isaiah, the son of Amos, did see concerning Moab, concerning Damascus, concerning Egypt, concerning the wilderness of the sea, or those nations of northern Europe where they have to dike out the water in order to till the land, concerning the valley of vision which is Palestine and concerning Tyre." Right in the midst of these whose future is definitely prophesied, enclosed in a circle of the then known nations, a country and a people are described and prophesied that are not named.

This chapter 18 is admittedly a most difficult passage for the interpreter. It is one of the most obscure prophecies; the people to whom it is addressed, the person he sends, the ambassadors, the nations to whom they are sent are extremely doubtful. Most commentators pass it by with brief and inane words showing they have no idea of its meaning. In such translations, you may look for poor work in rendering the meaning of unknown words. In this respect, chapter 18 of Isaiah is one of the most inaccurate, awkward and indefinite translations of the Old Testament.

The Hebrew word "hoi erets" with which chapter 18 opens is a mistranslation. It is not an exclamation of "woe," but hailing for attention, i.e., "Ho" or "All hail." It is the same word used in the same sense in the 55th chapter of Isaiah, *"Ho, everyone that thirsteth,"* and the whole tenor of chapter 18 shows that it should be translated in the same manner there. The nation described is not one that is "meted out and trodden down." The tense is wrong. It is more accurately translated "That meteth out and treadeth down." It is not "scattered and peeled" or "spread out and polished" but "tall and smooth." Its land has not been "spoiled" or "divided" by rivers, but "quartered."

ISAIAH'S VISION OF OUR COUNTRY
CHAPTER 18

1 – *Woe to the land shadowing with wings, which is beyond the rivers of Ethiopia:*

2 – *That sendeth ambassadors by the sea, even in vessels of bulrushes upon the waters, saying, Go, ye swift messengers, to a nation scattered and peeled, to a people terrible from their beginning hitherto; a nation meted out and trodden down, whose land the rivers have spoiled!*

3 – *All ye inhabitants of the world, and dwellers on the earth, see ye, when he lifteth up an ensign on the mountains; and when he bloweth a trumpet, hear ye.*

4 – *For so the Lord said unto me, I will take my rest, and I will consider in my dwelling place, like a clear heat upon herbs, and like a cloud of dew in the heat of harvest.*

5 – *For afore the harvest, when the bud is perfect, and the sour grape is ripening in the flower, he shall both cut off the sprigs with pruning hooks and take away and cut down the branches.*

6 – *They shall be left together unto the fowls of the mountains, and to the beasts of the earth: and the fowls shall summer upon them, and all the beasts of the earth shall winter upon them.*

7 – *In that time shall the present be brought unto the Lord of hosts of a people scattered and peeled, and from a people terrible from their beginning hitherto; a nation meted out and trodden under foot, whose land the rivers have spoiled, to the place of the name of the Lord of hosts, the mount Zion.*

Let us give attention to the specific points of description and see if Isaiah does not clearly designate America and the government of the United States.

ONE: *"Woe to the land shadowing with wings, which is beyond the rivers of Ethiopia."*

In this first verse of Isaiah 18, we find two words which identify the land in question. Since the chapter is not addressed to any land by name, while the other chapters in the Book are specially addressed, we can conclude the land in question to be a land unknown to Isaiah's time and general territory. This land will be *"beyond the rivers of Ethiopia."* The "rivers" referred to would be the Nile and its tributaries. However, the word "beyond" in Hebrew means "west." When we look today at a map, the top is north, the bottom south, the right is east and the left is west. – Not so in biblical times. The Hebrews faced the sunrise. They looked eastward. "Before" meant east; "behind" or "beyond" meant west. His right arm pointed south, and his left arm pointed to the north. "Beyond" the rivers of Ethiopia (land of Cush) meant over his shoulder west. Let Isaiah stand in Jerusalem, face the sunrise and describe the land beyond (west) the rivers of Ethiopia. Following that line of latitude from Jerusalem, west, you will see no country till you strike America at the coasts of South Carolina and Georgia.

The second identification, found in the first verse of Isaiah 18, is the expression *"shadowing with wings,"* which may be rendered "over-shadowing wings" or "outstretched" (wings). Several inferences can be drawn from this expression:

1. It referred to the geographical conformation of the new continent; for a large map of North and South America very much resembles the expanded wings of a great eagle.

2. It is suggestive of the fact that it was a country shadowed or concealed till God was ready for its discovery.

3. It foretold the "spread eagle," the symbol of Americanism. While other countries have the eagle as their national emblem, no other country has the eagle with outstretched wings. Mexico has an eagle with closed wings; Germany has an eagle with closed wings; Russia

has an eagle grasping a round globe – representing the whole earth – and an arrow to conquer the earth with war. The United States has an eagle with spread wings, and therefore, it is actually a "land of outstretched wings."

It was Divine Providence that the bald eagle was selected as the emblem of the United States (as a nation), and there is a deep truth hidden under this symbol that is scripturally applicable to Israel's deliverance and ultimate repentance. *"And to the woman* [Israel] *were given two wings of a great eagle, that she might fly into the wilderness, into her place, where she is nourished. . ."* (Rev. 12:14) The prophet Micah described the idolatry of Israel and the incurable wound of Judah, but speaks of a time when *"Yet will I bring an heir unto thee, O inhabitant of Mareshah; he shall come unto Adullam* [resting place] *the glory of Israel. Make thee bald* [repent], *and poll thee for thy delicate children; enlarge thy baldness* [baldness is the symbol for repentance] *as the eagle; for they are gone into captivity from thee."* (Micah 1:15,16)

The outstretched wings, like a mother bird protecting her brood under her wings, also foreshadowed a nation that would serve as a refuge for all oppressed people of the earth. Since the world began there has never been any country, except America, that from its beginning offered a welcome and hospitality to the downtrodden and suffering people of every part of the world for the purpose of giving them religious freedom and civil liberty.

TWO: *"That sendeth ambassadors by the sea, even in vessels of bulrushes upon the waters . . ."*

Two points need to be noted here. First, the ambassadors are sent "by sea." The word "ambassadors" means men who travel on business for the government, not those who travel for pleasure or profit. For over 150 years, all our ambassadors went by water to Europe, Asia, Australia, even to South and Central America. Only two countries, Canada and Mexico, did our representatives not have to cross the sea to arrive at their assignments.

Second, when the translators of the King James Version (1611) came to a Hebrew compound word, "water-drinking vessels," they had no idea what it meant, so they looked around for something that grew out of the water and guessed "bulrushes, cattails, flags, papyrus"; hence the words "vessels of bulrushes." There were Hebrew words for each of those plants, but none were used or meant. However, "vessels that drink" is a perfect description of our modern-day steamship, which was not even dreamed of in Isaiah's time or perceived by the King James translators. The words, *"water drinking vessels upon the waters"* are a picture of the ocean liners, pumping up water, distilling it, turning it into steam to propel its crew, passengers and cargo unto all lands. Isaiah was looking down the ages and seeing the time when America would be exercising a controlling power throughout the world by sending all its ambassadors, soldiers and sailors by vessels that "drink up water" and make steam to propel them on all the waters of the world.

THREE: *"Go, ye swift messengers, to a nation scattered and peeled, to a people terrible from their beginning hitherto; . . ."*

The word "scattered" is from the Hebrew "mashak" meaning "drawn out" or tall. The word "peeled" is from the Hebrew "marat," meaning "to pluck off hair" or "smooth-shaven." It is evident that the prophet had a vision of a land wherein the men were tall like trees with the bark peeled off; the best translation available is "tall and clean-shaven."

The year 1000 A.D. was the first discovery of America by the Norsemen, who came over to Canada and Massachusetts from Greenland. They found a race inhabiting this continent, "tall and smooth." The Indians were taller than the Asians or Europeans and were without beards. The description of this land, possessed originally by a people "terrible from their beginning," is a true description of the fierce and warlike Indians found in this new world, broken up into numerous tribes, dispersed without order over the whole country and wasted by continual tribal wars.

It is noteworthy that Isaiah's description of a *"people tall and smooth"* and *"terrible from their beginning"* not only fits the original inhabitants of America, but its later people as well. In the World War of 1914, America mobilized an army of three million soldiers that averaged five feet, eleven inches in height. This was the tallest army the world had ever seen, and there was not a full beard among them. Convinced they were fighting a "just war," they were a "terror" unto the enemy. Even in the process of being born, our nation whipped the mightiest nation of the known world (*"terrible from their beginning"*) and fought victorious with Mexico, Spain, Germany and Japan. We have never been defeated in the defense of our own lands or the freedom of the seas. The word "onward" in the prophecy suggests that

America will never be conquered from without down to the end of the ages.

FOUR: "*. . . a nation meted out and trodden under foot . . .*"

The word "*meteth*" out is from the Hebrew "qav-qav" meaning "line-line." "Treadeth down" (or trodden down – King James) is from the Hebrew "Mebusoh," which may be rendered "trodden under foot." Putting them together, a literal translation would be a land "measured out under the treading" – that is a land measured out by lines under feet. This is descriptive of our process of surveying, which began in 1800 and in which our land became literally a checker-board of sections. About the same time that Florida and Louisiana were taken into the Union and Ohio became a state, the government passed a law that all public lands should be surveyed by the north star, a base line run east and west, and all this land marked up into mile square sections. These sections were then subdivided into quarter sections of half-mile squares. No nation was ever so "meted" out in blocks before. All the countries of the earth, as in the division of the land under Joshua, surveyed and marked their land by local boundaries.

FIVE: "*. . . whose land the rivers have spoiled, . . .*"

The Revised Version translates "*whose land the rivers divide.*" However, the word "spoiled" is from the Hebrew "baza" meaning "to cleave," a term used in the ritual of sacrifice where an animal is hung up and divided into four quarters. The word should be rendered, literally, "quartered." An examination of all nations of the world shows only one, the United States, that is quartered by rivers. The Mississippi River takes its rise near the Canadian border and cuts right down to the Gulf of Mexico, dividing our land into halves. On the Pacific Coast side is the Columbia River. Follow it upward to its junction with the Snake River; follow that upward into close proximity with the source of the Missouri River, which starts in Montana and meanders eastward into the Mississippi, dividing the west into halves. On the Atlantic Coast side begin with the Ohio River and follow it eastward to Pittsburgh and its junction with the Monongahela River that runs by McKeesport, then follow eastward the Younghiogheny River where at Glenco, Pennsylvania, it becomes the Castleman River. Go on up-stream till Wills Creek branches off and takes its source where the Potomac begins and runs to the Bay and the Atlantic, and you have the eastern half of the nation divided in two. Thus the whole land is "quartered by rivers." One cannot find any other land on earth divided in this way, into four sections: Northeast, Northwest, Southeast, Southwest, by rivers.

SIX: *"All ye inhabitants of the world, and dwellers on the earth, see ye, when he lifteth up an ensign on the mountains; and when he bloweth a trumpet, hear ye."*

In this prophetic third verse we find use of the words "ensign" and "trumpet," which are symbols of war. Isaiah saw America lift up its ensign on the mountain (nation) and blow the trumpet – a declaration of war. Twice when America "declared" war, most of the nations of the world "took heed" and became involved. In each case our nation took leadership in making the terms and the regulations for managing and adjusting the varied claims of the nations.

SEVEN: *"For so the Lord said unto me, I will take my rest, and I will consider in my dwelling place like a clear heat upon herbs, and like a cloud of dew in the heat of harvest."*

"For afore the harvest, when the bud is perfect, and the sour grape is ripening in the flower, he shall both cut off the sprigs with pruning hooks, and take away and cut down the branches."

"They shall be left together unto the fowls of the mountains, and to the beasts of the earth: and the fowls shall summer upon them, and all the beasts of the earth shall winter upon them."

These words of Isaiah 18:4-6 are so highly figurative (Eastern) that it is difficult for the Western mind to understand their meaning. A possible interpretation is that the Prophet is speaking of a nation blessed with fertile soil, sunshine and showers (clouds of dew), favorable for cultivation and bountiful harvest, and natural resources favorable to national productivity. But in verse 5, branches of ill omen (*"sprigs"*) will spring up with the luxurious prosperity that comes to the country.

However, a time of cleansing (for our nation) is indicated as *"afore the harvest."* Matt. 13:39 tells us that the harvest is the consummation of the age. So, at the close of the age, those worthless evil branches are to be pulled off and exposed, and left for the predatory external forces, here called *"fowls"* and *"beasts,"* to destroy.

EIGHT: *"In that time shall the present be brought unto the Lord of hosts of a people scattered and peeled, and from a people terrible from their beginning hitherto; a nation meted out and trodden under foot, whose land the rivers have spoiled, to the place of the name of the Lord of hosts, the mount Zion.*"

In this closing verse we are shown the outcome of the cleansing. As in the parable of the wheat and the tares, the removal of the wicked forces is shown to precede the time that the people turn to God. Also in verse 7, we find that this Christian land, the "*place of the name of the Lord of hosts*," bears one name in the passage, the name of "*the mount Zion.*"

Beginning with the 40th chapter of Isaiah, we again find prophecies concerning America-Israel. Chapter 40 is an acknowledgment that God is keeping an eye on our forefathers according to His covenant, although they had been scattered into far distant countries: to the West, to the East, to the North and to the South (Gen. 28:14). The essence of the chapter is expressed in the lines: "*Comfort ye, comfort ye, my people, saith your God . . . Have ye not known? Have ye not heard? Hath it not been told you from the beginning? . . . It is he that sitteth upon the circle of the earth.*" This text was the theme of Handel's wonderful oratoria, "The Messiah," which would mean a great deal more to the listeners if they recognized that its comforting stanzas are actually addressed to Israel's race.

If one studies carefully Isaiah's words, he will discover that God is speaking to Israel in New Testament times, far away from Old Palestine. From the 41st chapter onward, God addresses His people in the "appointed place," in the Islands of the West and in America: "*Keep silence before me, O islands; and let the people renew their strength; let them come near; then let them speak: let us come near together to judgment. Who raised up the righteous man from the east, called him to his foot, gave the nations before him, and made him rule over kings? He gave them as the dust to his sword, and as driven stubble to his bow . . . But thou, Israel, art my servant, Jacob, whom I have chosen, the seed of Abraham my friend . . . Fear not, thou worm Jacob, and ye men of Israel; I will help thee, saith the Lord, and thy redeemer, the Holy One of Israel.*"

In the 42nd chapter of Isaiah, God asks the question: "*Who is blind but my servant*"? Yet He is pleased for His righteousness sake: "*Behold my servant, whom I uphold; mine elect, in whom my soul delighteth; I have put my spirit upon him: he shall bring forth judgment to the Gentiles* [nations] . . . *I the Lord have called thee in righteousness, and will hold thine hand, and will keep thee, and give thee for a covenant of the people, for a light of the Gentiles; To open the blind eyes, to bring out the prisoners from the prison, and them that sit in darkness out of the prison house . . . Hear, ye deaf; and look, ye blind, that ye may see. Who is blind, but my servant? or deaf, as my messenger that I sent? Who is blind as he that is perfect, and blind as the Lord's servant? Seeing many things, but thou observest not; opening the ears, but he heareth not. The Lord is well pleased for his righteousness' sake; he will magnify the law, and make it honourable."*

In the 43rd chapter we read: *"But now thus saith the Lord that created thee, O Jacob, and he that formed thee O Israel, Fear not: for I have redeemed thee, I have called thee by thy name; thou art mine. When thou passeth through the waters, I will be with thee; and through the rivers, they shall not overflow thee; when thou walkest through the fire, thou shalt not be burned; neither shall the flame kindle upon thee . . . Even every one that is called by my name: for I have created him for my glory, I have formed him; I have made him. Bring forth the blind people that have eyes, and the deaf that have ears . . . Ye are my witnesses, saith the Lord, and my servant whom I have chosen: . . . This people have I formed for myself; they shall shew forth my praise."*

Chapter 49 addresses Israel as having been appointed by God as His stewards and witnesses; to be a servant nation unto Him; to colonize the earth; and to be a channel of blessing to all nations of the earth. *"Listen O isles, unto me; and hearken, ye people, from far; . . . Thou art my servant, O Israel, in whom I will be glorified . . . I will also give thee for a light to the Gentiles* [nations], *that thou mayest be my salvation unto the end of the earth . . . Thus saith the Lord, In an acceptable time have I heard thee, and in a day of salvation have I helped thee: and I will preserve thee, and give thee for a covenant* [Brith] *of the people, to establish the earth, to cause to inherit the desolate heritages* [America]; *That thou mayest say to the prisoners, Go forth; to them that are in darkness, Shew yourselves. They shall feed in the ways, and their pastures shall be in all high places . . . Behold I have graven thee upon the palms of my hands; thy walls are continually before me."*

Isaiah makes it clear that God is speaking to the "Lost Tribes of Israel" in these words: *"Thus saith the Lord, Where is the bill of your mother's divorcement, whom I have put away? or which of my creditors is it to whom I have sold you? Behold, for your iniquities have ye sold yourselves, and for your transgressions is your mother put away."* (Isaiah 50:1) Israel, Jehovah's wife of the Old Testament, had sold herself, was divorced from Him, and is to be brought under the influence of the New Covenant (accept Christianity).

During the Christian dispensation, Lost Israel was to possess certain "marks" of identification. These God-given marks are very many, and while the following list is not exhaustive, it constitutes a chain of evidence utterly impossible to ignore.

1. **Israel to be a great and mighty nation.**
   Gen. 12:2; 18:18; Deut. 4:7,8

2. **Israel to have multitudinous seed.**
   Gen. 13:16; 15:5; 22:17; 24:60; 26:4,24; 28:3,14; 32:12; 49:22; Isa. 10:22; Hos. 1:10; Zech. 10:7,8

3. **Israel to spread abroad to the West, East, North and South.**
   Gen. 28:14; Isa. 42:5,6

4. **Israel to have a new home.**
   II Sam. 7:10; I Chron. 17:9

5. **Israel's home to be north-west of Palestine.**
   Isa. 49:12; Jer. 3:18

6. **Israel to live in islands and coasts of the earth.**
   Isa. 41:1; 49:1-3; 51:5; Jer. 31:7-10

7. **Israel to become a company of nations.**
   Gen. 17:4-6,15,16; 35:11; 48:19; Eph. 2:12

8. **Israel to have a Davidic King (a perpetual monarchy within Israel).**
   II Sam. 7:13,19; I Chron. 22:10; II Chron. 13:5; Psa. 89:20,37; Eze. 37:24; Jer. 33:17,21,26

9. **Israel to colonize and spread abroad.**
   Gen. 28:14; 49:22; Deut. 32:8; 33:17; Psa. 2:8; Isa. 26:15; 27:6; 54:2; Zech. 10:8,9

10. **Israel to colonize the desolate place of the earth.**
    Isa. 35:1; 43:19,20; 49:8; 54:3; 58:11,12

11. **Israel to lose a colony, then expand, demanding more room.**
    Isa. 49:19,20

12. **Israel to have all the land needed.**
    Deut. 32:8

13. **Israel to be the first among the nations.**
Gen. 27:29; 28:13; Jer 31:7

14. **Israel to continue as a nation for ever.**
II Sam. 7:16,24,29; I Chron. 17:22-27; Jer. 31:35-37

15. **Israel's home to be invincible by outside forces.**
II Sam. 7:10; Isa. 41:11-14

16. **Israel to be undefeatable – defended by God.**
Num. 24:8,9; Isa. 15-17; Micah 5:8-9

17. **Israel to be God's instruments in destroying evil.**
Jer. 51:20; 51:19-24; Dan. 2:34,35

18. **Israel to have a land of great mineral wealth.**
Gen. 49:25,26; Deut. 8:9; 33:15-19

19. **Israel to have a land of great agricultural wealth.**
Gen. 27:28; Deut. 8:7,9; 28:11; 33:13,14,28

20. **Israel to be rich by trading.**
Isa. 60:5-11; 61:6

21. **Israel to be envied and feared by all nations.**
Deut. 2:25; 4:8; 28:10; Isa. 43:4; 60:10,12; Micah 7:16,17; Jer. 33:9

22. **Israel to lend to other nations, borrowing of none.**
Deut. 15:6; 28:12

23. **Israel to have a new name.**
Isa. 62:2; 65:15; Hos. 2:17

24. **Israel to have a new language.**
Isa. 28:11 (The Bible, by means of which God speaks now to Israel, is English not Hebrew.)

25. **Israel to possess the gates of her enemies.**
Gen. 22:17

26. **Israel to find the aborigines diminishing before her.**
Deut. 33:17; Isa. 60:12; Jer. 31:7-10

27. **Israel to have control of the seas.**
Deut. 33:19; Num. 24:7; Psa. 89:25; Isa. 60:5 (F. Fenton translates this last, "when rolls up to you all the wealth of the sea." That could not be unless Israel controlled it.)

28. **Israel to have a new religion (New Covenant).**
    Heb. 8:10-13; 9:17; Matt. 10:5-7; Luke 1:77; 2:32; 22:20;
    John 11:49-52; Gal. 3:13

29. **Israel to lose all trace of her lineage.**
    Isa. 42:16-19; Hos. 1:9,10; 2:6; Rom. 11:25

30. **Israel to keep the Sabbath for ever (one day in seven set aside).**
    Ex. 31:13,16,17; Isa. 58:13,14

31. **Israel to be called the sons of God (i.e., accept Christianity).**
    Hos. 1:10-11

32. **Israel to be a people saved by the Lord.**
    Deut. 33:27-29; Isa. 41:8-14; 43:1-8; 44:1-3; 49:25,26;
    52:1-12; 55:3-10,13; Jer. 46:27,28; Eze. 34:10-16; Hos. 2:23;
    13:9-14; 14:4,6

33. **Israel to be the custodians of the Oracles (Scriptures) of God.**
    Psa. 147:19,21; Isa. 59:21

34. **Israel to carry the Gospel to all the world.**
    Gen. 28:14; Isa. 43:10-12 (witnesses), 21; Micah 5:7

35. **Israel to be kind to the poor and set slaves free.**
    Deut. 15:7,11; Psa. 72:4; Isa. 42:7; 49:9; 58:6

36. **Israel to be the heir of the world.**
    Rom. 4:13

37. **Israel to be God's Glory.**
    Isa. 46:13; 49:3; 60:1,2

38. **Israel to possess God's Holy Spirit as well as His Word.**
    Isa. 44:3; 59:21; Hag. 2:5

39. **Israel to be God's Heritage, formed by God, for ever.**
    Deut. 4:20; 7:6; 14:2; II Sam. 7:23; I Kings 8:51,53; Isa. 43:21;
    54:5-10; Hos. 2:19,23; Joel 2:27; Micah 7:14-18

40. **Israel is the nation appointed to bring glory to God.**
    Isa. 41:8-16; 43:10,21; 44:23; 49:3

These are but a few of the "marks," or "signs," God has given in His Word by which we may know and recognize His lost people. None of the nations of the earth respond to all these identifications except the Anglo-Saxon-Celtic and kindred peoples under the leadership of the

United States of America (Manasseh) and Great Britain (Ephraim). Joseph (the birthright nation) was the recipient of all the preceding marks. By inheritance, his two sons, Ephraim and Manasseh, are found possessing them all. While Israelites remain in other countries, many came in separate migrations to America as Britains, Germans, Scandinavians and other national names. Thus America (one out of many) is representative of the whole House of Jacob.

BATTLE HYMN OF THE REPUBLIC

Mine eyes have seen the glory of the coming of the Lord;
He is trampling out the vintage where the grapes of wrath are stored;
He hath loosed the fateful lightning of His terrible swift sword:
His truth is marching on.

I have seen Him in the watch-fires of a hundred circling camps;
They have builded Him an altar in the evening dews and damps;
I have read His righteous sentence by the dim and flaring lamps:
His day is marching on.

I have read a fiery gospel writ in burnished rows of steel,
"As ye deal with my contemners, so with you my grace shall deal;
Let the Hero, born of woman, crush the serpent with his heel,
Since God is marching on."

He has sounded forth the trumpet that shall never call retreat;
He is sifting out the hearts of men before his judgment-seat;
O, be swift, my soul, to answer Him! be jubilant my feet;
Our God is marching on.

In the beauty of the lilies Christ was born across the sea,
With a glory in His bosom that transfigures you and me;
As He died to make men holy, let us die to make men free,
While God is marching on.

(CHORUS)
Glory, glory, hallelujah!
Glory, glory, hallelujah!
Glory, glory, hallelujah!
His truth is marching on.

Howe

AMERICA'S DESTINY

The belief that America has been providentially chosen for a special destiny has roots in the American past. It is by no means a belief that has been given up in this secular age. Such a belief is the focus of American sacred ceremonies, the inaugural addresses of our presidents and the sacred Scriptures of the civil religion. This American destiny, under God, is at the heart of the attempt by contemporary Americans to understand their nation's responsibility at home and abroad. Our responsibility in these matters is deepened because our forefathers (Israel) were the people with whom God made His unalterable Covenant.

The concept of a "chosen nation" is found in the Bible in the narration of the events occurring at the Red Sea when the Hebrew people were saved from the wrath of the Egyptians. *"For thou art an holy people unto the Lord thy God: the Lord thy God hath chosen thee to be a special people unto himself, above all people that are upon the face of the earth. The Lord did not set his love upon you, nor choose you, because ye were more in number than any people; for ye were the fewest of all people. But because the Lord loved you, and because he would keep the oath which he had sworn unto your fathers, hath the Lord brought you out with a mighty hand and redeemed you out of the house of bondmen, from the hand of Pharaoh king of Egypt."* (Deut. 7:6-8)

The early Pilgrims came to America with the biblical awareness of God guiding them to an "appointed" land where they would form a nation with a divine mission to the whole world. Governor John Winthrop stated it clearly in 1630: "The God of Israel is among us . . . We shall be as a city upon a hill." This idea influenced public opinion in the eighteenth century and continues to be a part of America's self-image today.

The landing of our Pilgrim forefathers on Plymouth Rock, November 21, 1620, was no mere accident. This was Joseph's land, and of it the patriarch Jacob spoke when he said: *"Joseph is a fruitful bough, even a fruitful bough by a well; whose branches run over the wall."* (Gen. 49:22) When the Pilgrims established their first colonies on this shore they found it a great wilderness, and it is spoken of in many places as "the wilderness." In the Book of Revelation, we find Israel fleeing into the wilderness to a place prepared by God, a place where Israel would dwell in safety. Also we find the following verse concerning Israel's sojourn in the writings of Hosea: *"Therefore, behold, I will allure her, and bring her into the wilderness, and speak comfortably unto her."* (Hosea 2:14)

We do not know how many of the Founding Fathers considered the possibility that some of the post-biblical nations were descendants of the exiled nations of Israel, but many of them were obviously caught up with the idea. This idea, especially strong in New England, appeared in many sermons in the eighteenth century:

"Congress put at the head of this spirited army the only man [Washington] on whom the eyes of all *Israel* were placed. Posterity, I apprehend, and the world itself, inconsiderate and incredulous as they may be of the dominion of Heaven, will yet do so much justice to the divine moral government as to acknowledge that this American *Joshua* was raised up by God, and divinely formed, by a peculiar influence of the Sovereign of the universe, for the great work of leading the armies of this American *Joseph* (now separated from his brethren), and conducting this people through the severe, the arduous conflict, to liberty and independence.

"Already does the new constellation of the United States begin to realize this glory. It has already risen to an acknowledged sovereignty among the republics and kingdoms of the world. And we have reason to hope, and, I believe, to expect, that God has still greater blessings in store for this *vine* which his own right hand hath planted, to make us high among the nations in praise, and in name, and in honor." (Rev. Ezra Stiles, 1783) The "vine" Stiles referred to (planted by God) is of the vineyard of which Isaiah wrote: *"For the vineyard of the Lord of Hosts is the house of Israel."*

Samuel Langdon, a New England Congregational minister (and president of Harvard from 1774 until 1780), in urging the ratification of the federal Constitution, preached a sermon titled, "The Republic of the Israelites An Example to the American States." In his sermon, Langdon detailed evidences of God's providence in the events of American history and prescribed ways to "make a wise improvement" of what God had granted to *"New Israel."*

Langdon goes on to recommend the laws of Moses for the law of the land, and explains the separation and yet interdependence of the moral laws of the Bible upon the civil laws of the state. He also compares the 12 tribes of Israel to the 13 colonies of the United States. (We have shown previously that Israel was also divided into 13 hereditary tribes, because Joseph's share was equally given to his two sons, Ephraim and Manasseh – Joshua 14:4).

Rev. Nicholar Street, in a sermon preached at East Haven, Connecticut (April 1777), drew on similarities between biblical Israel and America-Israel. Britain was compared to "Egypt," and characters in the Bible were given contemporary counterparts. America is likened to the wilderness the Israelites found themselves in after being "led out of the land of Egypt by the hand of Moses." Street describes Israel's trials and hardships in the wilderness: "We see that God kept the children of Israel in the wilderness for many years after He had delivered them from the hand of Pharaoh, on the account of their wickedness. He led them so long in the wilderness to humble and prove them . . . one trial after another . . . so our trials in this wilderness state are bringing out our corruptions . . . pride . . . selfishness . . . covetousness . . . ingratitude . . . rebellion . . . impatience . . . distrust . . . of God and his providence. All these come flowing forth from the midst of us under our trials in as conspicuous a manner as they did from the children of Israel in the wilderness."

Lyman Beecher (father of Harriet Beecher Stowe, authoress of *Uncle Tom's Cabin*), famed New England clergyman and first president of Lane Theological Seminary (1832), in a speech titled "A Plea for the West," declared that the United States was "destined to lead the way of moral and political emancipation of the world . . . It is time she understood her high calling, and was harnessed for the work," and that many of the resources for that destiny lay in the West.

America's Founding Fathers spoke deliberately and persistently of America-Israel's destiny. Thomas Jefferson concluded his second inaugural address with these words: "I shall need . . . the favor of that Being in whose hands we are, who led our fathers, as Israel of old, from their native land and planted them in a country flowing with all the necessaries and comforts of life." According to Jefferson, America was to act as a model democratic Republic, thereby serving as "the world's best hope."

"I always consider the settlement of America with reverence and wonder, as the opening of a grand scene and design in Providence for the illumination of the ignorant, and the emancipation of the slavish part of mankind all over the earth." (A Dissertation on the Canon and Feudal Law – John Adams)

"No people can be bound to acknowledge and adore the invisible hand which conducts the Affairs of men more than the People of the United States. Every step, by which they have advanced to the character of an independent nation, seems to have been distinguished by some token of providential agency." (George Washington)

"The world has its eye upon America. The noble struggle we have made in the cause of liberty has occasioned a kind of revolution in the human segment. The influence of our example has penetrated the gloomy regions of despotism, and has pointed the way to enquiries which may shake it to its deepest foundations." (Alexander Hamilton)

Benjamin Franklin and many other men who founded our nation believed that God was intimately involved in the events of American history, and that "Divine Providence" was the force that moved the United States to liberty and eventually to direct the world to the same end.

Although our Founding Fathers did believe that America had been providentially chosen for a special destiny, they were deeply divided over the meaning of their national mission. The two basic versions of the chosen theme when applied to the relationship between America and the peoples of other countries are:

One: We are to be as a "light to the nations," which by force of example will positively influence other peoples and perhaps draw them to an American haven of freedom. This view of American destiny had its classic expression during the Revolution and the Constitutional Period, but it had been nursed by the Puritans of Massachusetts Bay and has appeared repeatedly in the course of American history.

Two: We are to actively win others to American principles and safeguard those principles around the world. This assumption undergirded the foreign-mission enterprises of the American churches during the late nineteenth and early twentieth centuries, and has stimulated and vindicated America's participation in foreign wars.

During the Philippine crisis (1900), Albert J. Beveridge, the Junior Senator from Indiana, delivered a Senate speech giving his views of American destiny. In his conclusion Beveridge asserted that "God marked the American people as His chosen nation to finally lead in the regeneration of the world . . . For God's hand was in it all. His plans were working out their glorious results . . . This is a destiny neither vague nor undesirable. It is definite, splendid and holy." (Congressional Record XXXIII - 1900)

One could go on and on quoting famous men in America's history that mysteriously suggest our descent was from Israel of old, and that America has a predestination. The cynic may dispute this assertion and claim it is just coincidental. But there are too many "coincidences" in our history that prove the existence of a prearranged plan on the part of God Almighty, indicating that He is guiding the Destiny of America.

The United States of America is a land of peaceful dwelling places. Within our borders men and women have been able to live in security, free from the foreign invasions that have swept over other lands from time to time throughout the years of our existence. Our national history has exemplified the Lord's appraisal that *"when a strong man armed keepeth his palace, his goods are in peace."* (Luke 11:21) But in our prosperity we have forgotten God and His warning that if we turn aside from the righteousness of His laws, we will no longer be blessed in our undertakings. Christianity has fallen into disfavor.

We have allowed the murky self-indulgency of psychology to replace the Ten Commandments and the Sermon on the Mount. As we traveled this road, from the light into the dark, our vision grew blurred and dim so that we now no longer clearly see the Christian way to serve our country and fulfill our mission to the world. In fact, we have come to a time when many people in the United States suggest that it is unconstitutional or undesirable to associate Almighty God with the political and governmental structure of our country.

The liberal in our midst has risen high above us, occupying seats of authority and issuing edicts of regimentation, with the result that the former era of prosperity is ending; freedom is being curtailed and personal liberty is being destroyed. Our constitutional right to own private arms is being infringed upon. Our children are being used as pawns in socialistic programs. Expressions of patriotism (displaying banners such as "God Bless America," singing patriotic songs, even pledging allegiance to the flag) is discouraged, if not prohibited, in some public schools in America. The grossest immorality is taught by some professors and when exposed is defended under the right of "academic freedom."

Our cities are hot-beds of crime and political graft. Our newsstands are full of filthy and indecent literature. The use of drugs has run rampant, and the use of alcohol is threatening to do likewise. Our courts of justice judge men by a double standard. We say, "This man who steals is honest, but this man who steals is a thief"; or, "These men are innocent until proven guilty, but these men are guilty until proven innocent." We watch in silence while self-serving accusations are treated with respect, but denials by the accused are treated with scorn. The "rights" of the criminal supersede the welfare of the victim. Killers are turned loose to kill again.

The very lifeblood of enterprise that formerly coursed freely through the veins of our economy, enabling men to provide wealth in abundance from forest, hill and mountain, is now being materially restricted. From the much that is now being accomplished by our labors, the tax-gatherer leaves us but little. Under our present system of taxation and interest we penalize the industrious and reward the shiftless; confiscate the property of the unfortunate making them subjects of charity, and then consider ourselves benevolent.

Under the debt-usury money system of the international bankers, administered in America by the private Federal Reserve Banking System, our national debt, both public and private, is over 9 trillion dollars. Approximately half of the average worker's time goes to pay federal, state and local taxes. (2007) When we falter under this hopeless burden – and we will – our entire economic system will collapse, as planned by those who would betray America to God-hating nations that now rule roughly half of the world.

Without exception all the prophets proclaim that the present age will end in turmoil and violence as the result of evil having come to fruition. This is becoming more evident day by day as violent men and aggressive nations move to bring their evil plans to realization. During this time of trouble the prophets of the Lord have declared that the very heaven and earth are to be shaken, for it is the day of God's fierce anger. God says: *"Yet once more I shake not the earth only, but also heaven. And this word, Yet once more, signifieth the removing of those things that are shaken, as of things that are made, that those things which cannot be shaken may remain."* (Heb. 12:26,27)

Jeremiah likens this coming world conflict, which will bring the age to a close, to the destructiveness of a whirlwind: *"Behold, the whirlwind of the Lord goeth forth with fury, a continuing whirlwind: it shall fall with pain upon the head of the wicked. The fierce anger of the Lord shall not return, until he have done it, and until he have performed the intents of his heart: in the latter days ye shall consider it."* (Jer. 30:23,24)

We now live in the latter days, and it is the time of His fury. But the Prophet also declared: "*At the same time, saith the Lord, will I be the God of all the families of Israel, and they shall be my people.*" (Jer. 31:1) So protection from the devastating tempest is promised Israel. However, this protection will only come when America understands and assumes her national responsibility before God to confess her transgressions against the laws of God, and re-institute those laws as the laws of the land.

Through the centuries, Israel has usually had to be chastised into repentance. Just as God used the Assyrians to chastise Israel, he is building up our enemies to bring us into national repentance. Ezekiel, in chapter 38, writes of the day when the forces of Gog (anti-christ) gather against Israel (America) saying: "*I will go up to the land of unwalled villages; I will go to them that are at rest, that dwell safely, all of them dwelling without walls, and having neither bars nor gates. To take spoil, and to take a prey; to turn thine hand upon the desolate places that are now inhabited, and upon the people that are gathered out of the nations, which have gotten cattle and goods, that dwell in the midst of the land.*" (Ezek. 38:11,12)

The people of our nation will be driven to their knees by coming events, and if they are to pray the prayer of the Prophet Joel, lined out for them, word for word, they must first acknowledge that they are God's servant people. Joel's instructions are: "*Let them say, Spare thy people, O Lord, and give not thine heritage to reproach, that the heathen would rule over them; wherefore should they say among the people, Where is their God*"? (Joel 2:17)

As a people, we are no more worthy than any other people. It may be, that because of our neglect of our "Heritage," we are less worthy than any other people. Nevertheless, we are the descendants of Jacob-Israel, of whom God said: "*Will I be the God of all the families of Israel, and they shall be my people.*" (Jer. 31:1) In spite of our unrighteousness and national rejection of God in this day, He will not alter His words: "*Thou art my people; and they shall say, Thou art my God.*" (Hosea 2:23) Even in the midst of tribulation and trouble, in the light of this Divine guarantee, we can exclaim with the Psalmist: "*The Lord of hosts is with us; the God of Jacob is our refuge.*" (Psalm 46:7)

Through Christ we were redeemed to fulfill His mission of salvation of the world: "*But you are a chosen generation, a royal priesthood, an holy nation, a peculiar people; that ye should shew forth the praises of him who hath called you out of darkness into his marvelous light; Which in time past were not a people, but are now the people of God: which had not obtained mercy, but now have obtained mercy."* (I Peter 2:9-10)

The day must come when America-Israel will give voice to the words spoken through the Prophet Hosea: *"Come and let us return unto the Lord: for he hath torn, and he will heal us; he hath smitten, and he will bind us up."* (Hosea 6:1) We await the day of which the Prophet Isaiah wrote: *"Arise, shine; for thy light is come, and the glory of the Lord is risen upon thee. For behold, the darkness shall cover the earth, and gross darkness the people: but the Lord shall arise upon thee, and his glory shall be seen upon thee . . . for the Lord shall be thine everlasting light, and the days of thy mourning shall be ended."* (Isa. 60:1,2,20)

Let us therefore give ear to the call and *"Arise, shine,"* so that the Glory of the Lord through us will be manifested unto all nations, and that by our example they may understand and know the blessings of righteousness. This is the purpose and the mission of us His people Israel, and the reason for God having "Chosen" us so that we might show forth His praise: *". . . I will also give thee for a light to the Gentiles* [nations], *that thou mayest be my salvation unto the end of the earth." (Isa. 49:6) "But ye are a chosen generation, a royal priesthood, a holy nation, a peculiar people; that ye should shew forth the praises of him who hath called you out of darkness into his marvelous light. Which in time past were not a people, but are now the people of God: which had not obtained mercy but now have obtained mercy."* (I Peter 2:9,10)

To many persons the true meaning of the name "Israel" is lost or obscured. The fallacy persists that the Israel people were chosen by

God as an object of favoritism. It is easy to believe that America is God's "New Israel" to support arrogant self-righteousness. It has been all too easy for some Americans to convince themselves that they have been chosen to be a free and powerful people, not because of God's purpose, but because they deserve election. The blessings of success, wealth and power are readily taken as signs of their having merited a special place in history.

Nevertheless, the people of Israel were chosen – for "service" and "responsibility." God called Israel to convey to all mankind the blessings of peace, happiness and true progress. While performing that service, God guaranteed to Israel the reward that every faithful servant should receive: the benevolence and protection of the Master. He placed His own name upon them, "Israel," meaning "sons ruling with God," and commanded them not to "take it in vain." That they did so and lost their name, is a matter of history. That they will again carry it – to God's honor and service – is clear from the Scriptures.

The Prophet Isaiah clearly explains Israel's latter day special mission to the world: "*. . . to undo the heavy burdens, and to let the oppressed go free, and that ye break every yoke*" (to free all mankind from all forms of bondage or slavery), "*. . . to deal thy bread to the hungry*" (eliminate hunger from the earth), "*. . . bring the poor that are cast out to thy house*" (provide a refuge for those homeless and oppressed). (Isa. 58:6,7)

The Christian Church and her leaders have failed to recognize America as God's people, Israel, though at the same time declaring that as Christians they are the sons of the Living God. This is exactly what Hosea states would be said of Israel just previous to the awakening to their identity. "*And it shall come to pass, that in the place where it was said unto them, Ye are not my people, there it shall be said unto them, Ye are the sons of the living God.*" (Hosea 1:10)

Ultimately, the "Novus Ordo Seclorum" will dawn as lasting peace will be established, and nations will learn war no more. America will then recognize her place in Bible prophecy and assume Israel's responsibilities, thus fulfilling Israel's Destiny as symbolized in the Great Seal of the United States.

THE STORY OF THE LIBERTY BELL

"Proclaim Liberty Throughout All the Land Unto All the Inhabitants thereof." These words were put on the first Liberty Bell at the suggestion of Mr. Isaac Norris in 1751, who was chairman of the committee which ordered the Bell from London. When the Bell arrived in Philadelphia in 1752 and was rung, it broke at the first stroke of the clapper. The Bell was recast and made heavier. The new Bell hung in the City Hall of Philadelphia most of the time, except when the British threatened that city. It was rung at every important event in the history of the colonies, and after 1776 in the history of our young Republic. It also tolled the death of Chief Justice John Marshall in 1835 and cracked again, never to be heard since.

Why did our Liberty Bell crack twice? Is it possible that it did not ring true and proclaim Liberty to all the inhabitants of America? The following explanation is taken from *America's Appointed Destiny* by Frederick Haberman:

"The famous inscription on it (Liberty Bell) was taken from the 10th verse of the 25th chapter of Leviticus, but it was only a small part of that verse, which reads: '*And ye shall hallow the fiftieth year, and proclaim liberty throughout all the land unto all the inhabitants thereof: it shall be a jubilee unto you; and ye shall return every man unto his possession, and ye shall return every man unto his family.*'"

The Liberty, of which Leviticus, chapter 25, verse 10 speaks, was based upon the people of ancient Israel and the people of America-Israel hallowing the fiftieth year as a Jubilee year. To understand what a Jubilee cycle of fifty years is, we must study the whole of the 25th chapter of Leviticus. In that chapter we will find that a Jubilee cycle consists of Seven Sabbatic cycles of seven years each plus one year. Every seventh year Israel was commanded not to plant or harvest, but give the land a rest; and every creditor was commanded by the Lord to make a release:

"*At the end of seven years, there shall be a releasing, and this is the kind of releasing. – Every possessor of mortgaged land which his neighbor has mortgaged shall release it, he shall have no claim against his neighbor or his brother, because it is a Release by the Ever-Living.*" (Deut. 15:1,2. Fenton Bible)

"*But if your brother becomes poor, and his hand fails among you . . . Take no usury or increase from him, but fear your God, and let your*

94

brother live with you. You shall not lend your money to him at usury, and you shall not lend him food at an increase; for I am your Ever-Living God, who brought you from the land of the Mitzeraim [Egypt] *to give you the land of Canaan, to be for you from the Ever-Living.*" (Lev. 25:35-38, Fenton Bible)

That is very strong language and hard teaching, and if our pastors ever heard it they tried to forget about it. They thought they did well enough to make the people keep the Ten Commandments: "*Thou shalt not steal*"; "*Thou shalt not commit adultery*"; "*Thou shalt not covet*"; and all the rest. But to expound that nobody has the right to collect interest or usury on a loan, and every seventh year all debts and mortgages must be cancelled, that sounded too Utopian even for our clergy.

Yet the prohibition of interest (which is usury) and the command to release all debts and mortgages every seventh year is as fundamental as the Ten Commandments. Those laws were given to curb and control man's natural tendency to collect more than his share of God's blessings, and to assure a just and equitable distribution of wealth to all inhabitants of the land.

It was upon those Divine laws that the Liberty was based which was to be proclaimed every 50th year: "Proclaim Liberty Throughout All the Land Unto All the Inhabitants thereof." – Liberty from debts, interest, bonds, and mortgages. But such Liberty the signers of our Declaration of Independence did not have in mind. The Liberty Bell could not ring out such Liberty to the people and therefore became mum.

IN GOD WE TRUST

Upon some of the United States coins there appears the motto, "In God We Trust." This motto was used for the purpose of suggesting to all peoples that the United States is not a "heathen" nation. The motto was first suggested by Rev. M. R. Watkinson of Ridleyville, Pennsylvania, in a letter to Salmon P. Chase, Secretary of the Treasury, dated November 13, 1861.

The letter stated, in part: "One fact touching our currency has hitherto been seriously overlooked. I mean the recognition of the Almighty God in some form in our coins. What if our Republic were now shattered beyond reconstruction? Would not the antiquaries of succeeding centuries rightly reason from our past that we were a heathen nation? . . . I have felt our national shame in disowning God as not the least of our present national disaster."

Under the date of November 20, 1861, Secretary Chase addressed the following words in a letter to the Director of the Mint at Philadelphia: "No nation can be strong except in the strength of God, or safe except in His defense. The trust of our people in God should be declared on our national coins. You will cause a device to be prepared without unnecessary delay with a motto expressing in the fewest and tersest words possible this national recognition."

In the course of implementing Secretary Chase's request, it was found that the Act of January 18, 1837 prescribed the mottoes and devices that should be placed upon the coins of the United States, so that nothing could be done without legislation. In December, 1863, the Director of the Mint submitted to Secretary Chase for approval designs for the new one, two, and three-cent pieces, on which it was proposed that one of the following mottoes should appear: "Our country; our God"; "God, our Trust."

Secretary Chase's reply on December 9, 1863 stated: "I approve your mottoes, only that on that (coin) with the Washington obverse, the motto should begin with the word 'our,' so as to read: 'Our God and our country.' And on that with the shield, it should be changed so as to read, 'In God we trust.'" Congress passed the Act of April 22, 1864 that contained provisions for the use of the motto "In God we trust," and it is upon the two-cent bronze piece that the motto first appeared.

The Act of March 3, 1865 made it lawful for the Director of the Mint, with the approval of the Secretary of the Treasury, to place the motto, "In God we trust" on such coins "as shall admit of the inscription thereon." Under this Act the motto was placed upon the double eagle, eagle, and half eagle, and also upon the dollar, half and quarter dollars in 1866. The Coinage Act of February 12, 1873 reaffirmed the motto to be inscribed on such coins "as shall admit of such motto."

When the double eagle and eagle of new design appeared in 1907, it was soon discovered that the religious motto had been omitted. In response to a general demand, Congress ordered it restored, and the Act of May 18, 1908 made mandatory its appearance upon all coins on which it had heretofore appeared. The motto appears on all gold and silver coins struck since July 1, 1908, with the exception of certain dimes. It was not mandatory upon the one-cent and five-cent coins, but could be placed thereon by the Secretary of the Treasury or the Director of the Mint with the Secretary's approval.

The Act of July 11, 1955 makes the appearance of the motto, "In God we trust," mandatory upon all coins of the United States. In that same year a constituent asked Representative Charles E. Bennett of Florida why that motto did not appear on all United States money, both coins and currency. After looking into the matter, Bennett introduced a bill requiring that all future issues of coins and currency bear the motto, which was approved by both the House of Representatives and the Senate.

Further official recognition of the motto is found in a joint resolution passed by the House on April 16 and the Senate on July 23, and became law with the President's approval on July 30, 1965. It read: "Resolved by the Senate and House of Representatives of the United States of America in Congress assembled, that the national motto of the United States is hereby declared to be 'In God we trust.'"

The House Judiciary Committee, which had considered the resolution and reported it favorably to Congress, had recognized that the phrase, "E. Pluribus Unum," had also "received wide usage in the United States," and the joint resolution did not repeal or prohibit its use as a national motto. In essence, "In God we trust" is the motto of the United States, while "E. Pluribus Unum" is a motto of the United States.

ACKNOWLEDGEMENT

This treatise is indebted to the U.S. Department of State for their permission to draw from the publication, *The Eagle and the Shield*, "A History of the Great Seal of the United States," by Richard S. Patterson and Richardson Dougall (published by the Office of the Historian, Bureau of Public Affairs, Department of State, under the auspices of the American Revolution Bicentennial Administration – 1978).

Special appreciation must be expressed to the Library of Congress and the National Archives, Washington, D.C. for their kind permission to reprint evolutionary illustrations of the Great Seal.

A large portion of the material incorporated in this treatise is taken from the works of Professor Charles A. L. Totten of Yale University. In 1909 Professor Totten was given recognition for his exhaustive study of the Great Seal by the United States Government in a brochure published by the Department of State. The following is the preface of the publication:

To the Honorable Philander C. Knox,
Secretary of State.

Sir: In 1892, when I was serving in your Department, by direction of Secretary James G. Blaine, I prepared an historical sketch of the seal of the United States, entitled, "The Seal of the United States: How it was Developed and Adopted," which the Department printed. It was prepared in a given time and was meagre; and since it appeared I have gathered additional information concerning the history of the seal, which I now have the honor to offer the Department, the edition of the monograph of 1892 being exhausted.

In 1897, Mr. Charles A. L. Totten published his two-volume work in New Haven, *Our Inheritance in the Great Seal of Manasseh, the United States of America; Its History and Heraldry, and its Signification unto the "Great People" thus Sealed*; and I take pleasure in acknowledging my indebtedness to Mr. Totten's book for much valuable information concerning the seal.

I have the honor to be, Sir,

Gaillard Hunt
Library of Congress, April 30, 1909.

GEORGE WASHINGTON
1732-1799
President from April 30, 1789 until March 4, 1797

Appendix A

George Washington's Vision
And Prophecy For
The United States of America

by John Grady, M.D.

The great British statesman and four times Prime Minister, William E. Gladstone, once proposed the creation of a grouping of pedestals for statues of history's most famous men. One pedestal stood higher than all the rest, and Gladstone was asked to identify the figure to be given the place of honor. Without a moment's hesitation, he named George Washington.

At the Continental Congress, meeting in Philadelphia, December 1799, one of Washington's finest military commanders, the famous cavalry general, Henry "Light-Horse Harry" Lee, then Congressman from Virginia (and later to become that state's governor), upon hearing of the death of our first president, rose to his feet and with tears in his eyes spoke for all Americans for all time when he said of Washington, "First in war, first in peace, and first in the hearts of his countrymen."

Many students of history consider George Washington to be the greatest man who ever lived. Certainly, he was the greatest American – a brilliant, educated, successful man who risked everything for the freedom of our country.

Washington was a man of great moral character. He was forthright, honest, charitable and a gentle man of quiet modesty and proper deportment – considerate, kind and courteous.

Washington was also a man of great talent. He was knowledgeable in agriculture, was a surveyor with an established reputation, and early in life became a land owner of some importance and considerable wealth.

He was held in such respect that at the age of 21 he was made a Major and Adjutant of the Virginia Militia, and so distinguished himself that at the age of 23 he was made Commander-in-Chief of the Frontier Forces of Virginia.

Washington had a commanding appearance. He was the most physically impressive of all of our Presidents, and in his prime stood over 6 feet 4 inches tall and was a lean and powerful 225 pounds. In addition, this handsome figure had a distinct military bearing.

Washington was appropriately described by colleagues and writers of the time as "...straight, tall, wide-shouldered, with head well shaped, large straight nose, penetrating blue-gray eyes, a long handsome face terminating in a good firm chin, clear fair skin, firm mouth, and a commanding countenance; with speech, movement and gestures which are agreeable, differential, engaging and graceful."

Most important of all, Washington was a man with a total sense of responsibility, unquestioned integrity and deep devotion to God.

Among the many outstanding men of leadership in the American Colonies, Washington stood out above all. Once the War for Independence began, he was quickly and logically chosen Commander-in-Chief of the Colonial Forces. Washington had the impossible task of taking a few thousand untrained volunteers and leading them against the armies of the world's greatest empire. Great Britain was a powerful and progressive nation with colonies and influence around the world, and she had mighty armies and fleets to defend her possessions. England could accurately boast that the sun never set upon her flag or the British Empire.

To add to the difficulties was the fact that the American Colonies were not united, were economically weak, had no standing army and no navy, and had only three million people, who were seriously divided as to whether or not to fight for freedom.

It is not known what percentage of the Colonists genuinely supported the cause for freedom. Many of those who opposed independence constantly gave help, comfort and support to the enemy. Probably no more than 3% of the people in the Colonies actually took part in the fight for American independence. Then, as now, apathy, self-interests, uncertainty and fear prevailed among a large portion of the population.

Once the Declaration of Independence had been signed and Washington's forces were pitted against the British, his army was so greatly outnumbered and so ill equipped that many thought him foolhardy to even attempt to fight the most powerful nation in the world. Seldom in all of history has such a task been undertaken under such unfavorable conditions. However, Patrick Henry in his famous "Give me liberty or give me death" speech hit directly upon his reasons for hoping for ultimate victory when he said, "God will raise up friends to fight our battles for us."

General Washington led his men with a passion, courage and fortitude that could come only from total dedication. When the Continental Congress did not, or could not, send the funds for his soldiers' supplies and salaries, Washington paid for them out of his own pocket. He gained and held the allegiance of his men because he was fair, firm, resolute and dedicated. Moreover, he was a devoutly Christian man who made no apology for prayer. He repeatedly called upon God for deliverance and victory in the struggle for freedom.

The cover paintings of George Washington kneeling in prayer in the snow-covered woods of Valley Forge are based on fact. He believed that God would lead him to victory, and anyone who has read his handwritten letters and documents cannot help but be impressed by his reliance on the Almighty and his deep belief in Divine Guidance.

Strengthened by a sense of duty and honor, driven by a love of freedom and a hunger for justice, sustained by faith and confidence in Divine Providence, George Washington would not fail. He would fulfill his destiny. This uncommon man would lead the colonial forces to victory, become the father of our country, be unanimously acclaimed our first President, and set the course for what was to become history's greatest nation.

Little wonder then that he was shown great favor by the God of our universe. As the prophets of old were shown the destiny of mankind, so was Washington shown the destiny of our nation. General Washington had an unusual and profound spiritual experience in Valley Forge. He was given a vision of such momentous importance that it prompts the writing of this paper and the dissemination of this information to all concerned Americans.

Washington told of the event shortly after it took place. It was repeated to his close confidantes and fellow patriots during the 22 years he lived after its occurrence. And it has been carried in print from time to time over the past 200 years. However, since spiritual experiences tend to be ignored by secular historians, it has remained at times an obscurity.

Thomas Jefferson best expressed the relationship between man's highest aspiration and the great Creator when he wrote, "God who gave us life, gave us liberty." Throughout history, as is well documented in Holy Scripture and readily attested to by millions of observant people, God has raised up individuals, usually temporal leaders, to fulfill the destiny of men and nations.

It is the personal opinion of this writer that God moulded, inspired and directed George Washington. He was, indeed, chosen to be a special man, at a special time, for a special purpose.

Various accounts of George Washington's vision and prophecy all agree in content. There have been only minor variations in some details as the story was repeated over the years by those to whom it was related by General Washington.

The place was Valley Forge in the cold and bitter winter of 1777. Washington's army had suffered several reverses and the situation was desperate. Food was scarce. The Continental Congress was not sending supplies or money. Some of the troops did not even have shoes to wear in the snow. Many soldiers were sick and dying from disease and exposure. Morale was at an all-time low, and there was great agitation in the Colonies against the continued effort to secure our freedom from England. Nevertheless, General Washington was determined to see the struggle through.

These are the words of a first-hand observer, Anthony Sherman, who was there and describes the situation: "You doubtless heard the story of Washington's going to the thicket to pray. Well, it is not only true, but he used often to pray in secret for aid and comfort from God, the interposition of whose Divine Providence brought us safely through the darkest days of tribulation.

"One day, I remember it well, when the chilly winds whistled through the leafless trees, though the sky was cloudless and the sun shown brightly, he remained in his quarters nearly all the afternoon alone. When he came out, I noticed that his face was a shade paler than usual. There seemed to be something on his mind of more than ordinary importance. Returning just after dusk, he dispatched an orderly to the quarters who was presently in attendance. After a preliminary conversation of about an hour, Washington, gazing upon his companion with that strange look of dignity which he alone commanded, related the event that occurred that day.

"This afternoon, as I was sitting at this table engaged in preparing a dispatch, something seemed to disturb me. Looking up, I beheld standing opposite me a singularly beautiful female. So astonished was

I, for I had given strict orders not to be disturbed, that it was some moments before I found language to inquire the cause of her presence. A second, a third and even a fourth time did I repeat my question, but received no answer from my mysterious visitor except a slight raising of her eyes.

"By this time I felt strange sensations spreading through me. I would have risen but the riveted gaze of the being before me rendered volition impossible. I assayed once more to address her, but my tongue had become useless, as though it had become paralyzed.

"A new influence, mysterious, potent, irresistible, took possession of me. All I could do was to gaze steadily, vacantly at my unknown visitor. Gradually the surrounding atmosphere seemed as if it had become filled with sensations, and luminous. Everything about me seemed to rarify, the mysterious visitor herself becoming more airy and yet more distinct to my sight than before. I now began to feel as one dying, or rather to experience the sensations which I have sometimes imagined accompany dissolution. I did not think, I did not reason, I did not move; all were alike impossible. I was only conscious of gazing fixedly, vacantly at my companion.

"Presently I heard a voice saying, 'Son of the Republic, look and learn,' while at the same time my visitor extended her arm eastwardly. I now beheld a heavy white vapor at some distance rising fold upon fold. This gradually dissipated, and I looked upon a strange scene. Before me lay spread out in one vast plain all the countries of the world – Europe, Asia, Africa and America. I saw rolling and tossing between Europe and America the billows of the Atlantic, and between Asia and America lay the Pacific.

"'Son of the Republic,' said the same mysterious voice as before, 'look and learn.' At that moment I beheld a dark, shadowy being, like an angel, standing, or rather floating, in mid-air between Europe and America. Dipping water out of the ocean in the hollow of each hand, he sprinkled some upon America with his right hand, while with his left hand he cast some on Europe. Immediately a cloud raised from these countries, and joined in mid-ocean. For a while it remained stationary, and then moved slowly westward until it enveloped America in its murky folds. Sharp flashes of lightning gleamed through it at intervals, and I heard the smothered groans and cries of the American people.

"A second time the angel dipped water from the ocean, and sprinkled it out as before. The dark cloud was then drawn back to the ocean, in whose heaving billows it sank from view. A third time I heard the mysterious voice saying, 'Son of the Republic, look and learn.' I cast my eyes upon America and beheld villages and towns and cities springing up one after another until the whole land from the Atlantic to the Pacific was dotted with them.

"Again, I heard the mysterious voice say, 'Son of the Republic, the end of the century cometh, look and learn.' At this the dark shadowy angel turned his face southward, and from Africa I saw an ill-omened spectre approach our land. It flitted slowly over every town and city of the latter. The inhabitants presently set themselves in battle array against each other. As I continued looking I saw a bright angel upon whose brow rested a crown of light, on which was traced the word 'Union,' bearing the American flag which he placed between the divided nation, and said, 'Remember ye are brethren.' Instantly, the inhabitants, casting from them their weapons, became friends once more, and united around the National Standard.

"And again I heard the mysterious voice saying, 'Son of the Republic, look and learn.' At this the dark shadowy angel placed a trumpet to his mouth, and blew three distinct blasts; and taking water from the ocean, he sprinkled it upon Europe, Asia and Africa. Then my eyes beheld a fearful scene: from each of these countries arose thick, black clouds that were soon joined into one. Throughout this mass there gleamed a dark red light by which I saw hordes of armed men, who, moving with the cloud, marched by land and sailed by sea to America. Our country was enveloped in this volume of cloud, and I saw these vast armies devastate the whole country and burn the villages, towns and cities that I beheld springing up. As my ears listened to the thundering of the cannon, clashing of swords, and the shouts and cries of millions in mortal combat, I heard again the mysterious voice saying, 'Son of the Republic, look and learn.' When the voice had ceased, the dark shadowy angel placed his trumpet once more to his mouth, and blew a long and fearful blast.

"Instantly a light as of a thousand suns shone down from above me, and pierced and broke into fragments the dark cloud which enveloped America. At the same moment the angel upon whose head still shone the word Union, and who bore our national flag in one hand and a sword in the other, descended from the heavens attended by legions of white spirits. These immediately joined the inhabitants of America, who I perceived were well nigh overcome, but who, immediately taking courage again, closed up their broken ranks and renewed the battle.

"Again, amid the fearful noise of the conflict, I heard the mysterious voice saying, 'Son of the Republic, look and learn.' As the voice ceased, the shadowy angel for the last time dipped water from the ocean and sprinkled it upon America. Instantly the dark cloud rolled back, together with the armies it had brought, leaving the inhabitants of the land victorious!

"Then once more I beheld the villages, towns and cities springing up where I had seen them before, while the bright angel, planting the azure standard he had brought in the midst of them, cried with a loud voice: 'While the stars remain, and the heavens send down dew upon the earth, so long shall the Union last.' And taking from his brow the crown on which was blazoned the word 'Union,' he placed it upon the Standard, while the people, kneeling down, said, 'Amen.'

"The scene instantly began to fade and dissolve, and I at last saw nothing but the rising, curling vapor I at first beheld. This also disappearing, I found myself once more gazing upon the mysterious visitor, who, in the same voice I had heard before, said, 'Son of the Republic, what you have seen is thus interpreted: Three great perils will come upon the Republic. The most fearful is the third, but in this greatest conflict the whole world united shall not prevail against her. Let every child of the Republic learn to live for his God, his land and the Union.' With these words the vision vanished, and I started from my seat and felt that I had seen a vision wherein had been shown to me the birth, progress, and destiny of the United States."

Thus ended General George Washington's vision and prophecy for the United States of America as told in his own words.

COMMENTARY

George Washington's vision has been published from time to time and is recorded in the Library of Congress. My purpose in relating this prophecy and the historical background of events surrounding it is to increase your understanding and motivation for the struggle ahead.

We are now moving rapidly into the third and greatest peril of Washington's revelation. The signs of its fulfillment are readily evident to all who are not blinded by apathy, overindulgence, or self-delusion.

Nations on every continent are now hostile to the United States. America has few friends left in the world and even fewer still who will have the strength or will to stand beside her in any future struggles.

In Washington's vision, he saw America attacked and invaded by vast military forces from Europe, Asia and Africa. He saw that with those forces there "gleamed a dark, red light" – the color and symbol of Communism. He saw our cities aflame (as a result of nuclear attack, burned by the invading enemy forces, or perhaps set afire by mobs fomenting anarchy and revolution), the whole nation devastated, and millions dying in mortal combat.

Then, at the point of the fiercest and final battle, the great angel, the guardian of this nation, descended from the heavens with legions of white spirits, who joined forces with the Americans and destroyed the invading armies.

There are several important points which should be recognized by every American who reads this:

(1) It is time for all Americans to heed the warning that the remnant have been carrying across this land for several decades. The people of this nation are entering a period of great trial and tribulation.

(2) America is the promised land and the Christian people of North America are God's chosen people. We will prevail because it is our destiny to prevail. But we have permitted corruption, perversion, immorality, greed, personal pleasure, and materialism to become our way of life. We have allowed men and women to occupy the highest positions of authority within our nation, who do not choose to uphold the biblical principles upon which our country was founded. We have reached such a point of degradation that we are even killing our own

unborn children – bringing about our own genocide. Therefore, because of immorality, loss of faith, and the abandonment of our God-centered heritage, America and her people will receive a chastisement of immeasurable ferocity.

(3) The events which you are reading about are neither fiction, a patriotic story, nor a series of simple historical happenings. The authenticity of Washington's revelation is clearly supported by a number of other prophecies over the past several hundred years, all pointing to a great "end times" battle in which the forces of almost the entire world are directed against the United States.

This is a cataclysmic demonstration of the power of God and the fact that His will shall not be frustrated and His plan shall not be denied. We Americans have accepted and enjoyed our many blessings and great bounty without gratitude; we have failed to understand and fulfill our special role as a nation. Consequently, we will soon feel the correction of God, which is our just punishment.

(4) George Washington, the greatest man ever to walk this continent, should serve as our example in these troubled times. Washington's selfless devotion to his Country, his total dedication to the Cause of Liberty, his blameless private life and high personal standards of morality and character—all made him universally loved and respected. He should be the hero and the model for every man and boy in America today.

General Washington was a man of principle, wisdom, determination, and great courage. He was a God-fearing man who prayed for direction, strength and support from the Almighty, and he accepted the purpose and destiny for which he was created.

Washington also had the courage to take up arms and physically fight for his God and his country. He did not expect other men or the Creator to do it for him, nor did he foolishly think that somehow God would pluck him from the scene so that he might avoid the hardships, suffering, and perhaps even death which were imminent. Good men, including dedicated Christians, have never escaped tribulation; but those, like Washington, who are prepared, are given the strength and courage to see it through.

Appendix B

Our Constitution, A Historical Review
by W. Clyde Odeneal

A constitution has been defined as the fundamental organic law or the principles of government of a nation, state, society, or other organized body of men, embodied in written documents, or implied in institutions and customs; also, a written instrument embodying such organic law. The British constitution is exemplified in the first part of this definition — the United States Constitution in the last part.

In order to understand our Federal Constitution, we must understand the character of the men who wrote it and their ancestors. From the time the English barons wrested Magna Charta from King John at Runnymede in 1215, until the 56 signers of the Declaration of Independence (all white and of British ancestry) mutually pledged to each other their lives, their fortunes and their sacred honor, our forebears were motivated by the urge for freedom under God.

The early settlers on the new continent of North America came and settled as subjects and colonists of the British crown. The first colony was at Jamestown, Virginia, in 1607. Later, in 1620, came the Mayflower passengers who wrote and signed the Mayflower Compact, which reads in part as follows:

"In the name of God, Amen! We, whose names are underwritten, the loyal subjects of our dread sovereign Lord, King James, by the grace of God, of Great Britain, France and Ireland, Defender of the Faith etc., have undertaken for the glory of God and the advancement of the Christian faith, and honor of our King and country, a voyage to plant the first colony in the northern parts of Virginia; do by these presents, solemnly and mutually, in the presence of God and of one another, covenant and combine ourselves together into a civil body politic for our better ordering and preservation."

The Mayflower carried the most precious cargo that ever sailed the sea. It was in the cabin of the Mayflower that the Compact was signed. Daniel Webster called the Compact the Seed Corn of the Constitution, and a century after its adoption Gladstone described the Constitution as "The most wonderful work ever struck off at a given time by the brain and purpose of man."

By 1776, about three million people were in the 13 colonies along the Atlantic coast. They had petitioned the king time after time for just and equitable laws, especially regarding taxation, but to no avail. Armed resistance became inevitable. The first Continental Congress met in Philadelphia on September 5, 1774.

Their Declaration of Rights and Grievances was ignored. The second Congress met on May 10, 1775, and voted to raise an army to resist England. George Washington was appointed Commander-in-Chief of the Continental army. The colonies were determined to be free, and on July 4, 1776, the Declaration of Independence was adopted.

The cornerstone of the Declaration is found in these words: "...that these United Colonies are, and of right ought to be, Free and Independent States." The emphasis was upon Free and Independent States.

The Articles of Confederation were proposed in 1778 and adopted in 1781. In these Articles, imperfect though they were, we see the forerunner of the Constitution, especially in the reserved rights of the States in the Second and Third Articles.

Now let's take a look at some of the men who composed the Constitutional Convention. The 55 delegates included lawyers, physicians, merchants, financiers, educators, planters, soldiers and statesmen. All were men of great ability, high character and undying courage. Twenty-five were college graduates. The oldest was Benjamin Franklin, 81 years, and the youngest was Jonathan Dayton, 26 years. The average age was about 43 years.

Their greatest asset was their heritage — generations of forebears who knew their law, their Bible and the extremes of government. They knew what it meant to live under a strong central government headed by a monarch. Their task was to devise a plan which would exclude rule by mob and dominance by tyranny.

The task was not easy; but if the problems were unusual, so were the delegates! They had not only a high degree of patriotism and dedication, but also what we now call "political know-how." They knew history and the science of government. But they represented 13 States with different backgrounds. About the only things the States had in common were their racial background, their desire to be free of the British crown, and their determination to retain their sovereignty.

The Convention met in May, 1787. George Washington presided. His greatness as a statesman was reflected in these words: "If, to please the people, we offer what we ourselves disapprove, how can we afterward defend our work? Let us raise a standard to which the wise and honest can repair; the event is in the hand of God."

In spite of the high plane of thought Washington set, the Convention seemed to make no progress. There was no harmony — only heated discussion and wrangling. At this point the immortal Franklin, printer, inventor, student, diplomat and statesman, arose to address the delegates. Among other inspiring things he said: "In this situation of this Assembly, groping as it were in the dark to find political truth, and scarce able to distinguish it when presented to us, how has it happened, Sir, that we have not hitherto once thought of humbly applying to the Father of Lights to illuminate our understandings"?

"I have lived, Sir, a long time, and the longer I live, the more convincing proofs I see of this truth—that God governs in the affairs of men. And if a sparrow cannot fall to the ground without his notice, is it probable that an empire can rise without his aid?...

"I therefore beg leave to move — that henceforth prayers imploring the assistance of Heaven, and its blessings on our deliberations, be held in this Assembly every morning before we proceed to business."

Without acting on the motion, from that time onward the Convention moved swiftly to the completion of its task.

The task was not merely to draw a Constitution. It was to write a document under which the States would delegate certain powers to the Federal Government while reserving all other powers to themselves and their people. Thus the Constitution delegated to the Federal Government only such posers as the right to collect taxes, pay debts and provide for the common defense—of the United States; to borrow; to regulate commerce with foreign nations and among the several States; to coin money; to provide for patents and copy rights; to declare war; and to raise and support an army.

In addition to the limited delegation of power, perhaps the factor that makes our Constitution a new creation, an original work, is the separation of powers of the three branches of government: Executive, Legislative and Judicial. Each branch or department was designed to work with the others but be free of the dominance of either. Sometimes we call this our "checks and balances." In any event, the idea was to prevent the emergence of a totalitarian government and to provide for a dual citizenship – that of the state and of the nation.

Unlike some State Constitutions, our Federal Constitution contains no statutory material. The "founding fathers," in their wisdom, were careful to see that their work embodied principles of government — not statutory enactments. For example, the Constitution fixes no salaries of public officials; makes no provision for the number of members of the legislative branch; and does not stipulate the number of justices the Supreme Court shall have.

Article I of the Constitution outlines the powers and duties of and limitations upon the Legislative Department, and provides for a Senate and House of Representatives.

Article II deals with the Executive Department and the President, determines the qualifications of the President and sets forth the powers and duties of the President. He shall be Commander-in-Chief of the Army and Navy; he shall from time to time give Congress information of the State of the Union, make recommendations to Congress, and on extraordinary occasions he can convene or adjourn Congress. The President must make an oath, or affirm, that he will preserve, protect and defend the Constitution.

Article III sets up the Judicial Department. Section I of this Article briefly reads: "The judicial power of the United States shall be vested in one supreme court, and in such inferior courts as the Congress may from time to time ordain and establish." The number of justices on the original Supreme Court was three. Congress increased it to nine. Congress could increase the number to 15, as President Franklin D. Roosevelt tried to persuade the Congress to do in 1937. Thus, in a way, Congress is made superior to the Court, for it can determine the size of the Court, fix the salaries of the justices and establish inferior courts and fix their salaries.

Article IV deals with the relation of states to each other and of the Federal Government to states and territories. Section 4 of this Article reads: "The United States shall guarantee to every state in this Union a Republican form of Government, and shall protect each of them against invasion; and on application of the Legislature, or of the Executive (when the Legislature cannot be convened) against domestic violence." There is nothing in the Constitution that gives the Executive, or any other department of the Federal Government, the right to "invade" a state to enforce a court decree.

Article V provides for amending the Constitution. It is interesting to note that this Article has a proviso which prevents any amendment designed to deprive a state of two Senators.

Article VI makes provision for national debts, defines supreme law of the land, requires oath or affirmation of all national and state officers to support the Constitution, and bans any religious test to hold office. Many constitutional lawyers and statesmen have felt that only in this Article did the founding fathers make a mistake — that part that makes treaties made under the authority of the United States a part of the "supreme law of the land." It was this loophole that Senator John Bricker wanted to correct by the Amendment he proposed.

Article VII provides the method for ratification. Although up to this point the Constitution was a model for dual citizenship, checks and balances and the preservation of freedom, it became obvious that without a "Bill of Rights" ratification could never be secured. The people of the states were jealous of their rights, and they feared too much power in a central government. They could not forget the tyrannies under King George and his predecessors.

The first ten amendments, which we call the Bill of Rights, were adopted and the ratification became finally a reality. Some students of the Constitution think the 9th and 10th Amendments were surplus. Even if they are right, these amendments especially show the determination of the people of the respective states to reserve all powers not expressly delegated.

"Article IX. The enumeration in the Constitution of certain rights shall not be construed to deny or disparage others retained by the people."

"Article X. The powers not delegated to the United States by the Constitution, nor prohibited by it to the states, are reserved to the states respectively, or to the people."

Under our Constitution we have a Republic— a representative form of government, both Federal and State—not a democracy.

Even including the first ten amendments, the Bill of Rights, and the questionable amendments following the War of 1861-65, the Constitution has had only 22 amendments in 175 years! During the first 125 years, we made the greatest progress of any nation in history and set the pace for the rest of the world to envy and emulate. We lived under constitutional guarantees of freedom from governmental interference, control and domination.

What has happened to our constitutional guarantees? These things: (1) Less love of freedom, which involves the people, (2) usurpation of authority by the Executive Department, (3) usurpation by the Supreme Court, and (4) failure of Congress to maintain its place in our system of checks and balances.

The adoption of the 16th Amendment, authorizing Congress to tax incomes from every source without apportionment among the several states, was the first great blow to the reserved rights of the states — far greater than the War of 1861-65. No limitation to tax was provided for and the people were led to believe that such was unnecessary as the tax would never exceed 2 or 3 percent!

So now as much as 91% of incomes are being taken as taxes in some instances. Money is power and when the government can take billions a year from individual incomes, it exercises more power. The lowest rate begins at 20 percent, and 50 percent of the income taxes collected each year comes from people making less than $15,000 a year.

The 17th Amendment, adopted May 31, 1913, was a step away from representative government in that it provides for the election of U.S. Senators by a vote of the people of each state, rather than by the State Legislatures. This Amendment enables petty politicians to seek the office of U.S. Senator, instead of the office seeking the man through the legislatures. Remember, Senators represent the States, not the people directly.

George Washington foresaw the possibility of usurpation and warned against it in his Farewell Address to the American People in these words: "If, in the opinion of the people, the distribution or modification of the constitutional powers be in any particular wrong, let it be corrected by an amendment in the way which the Constitution designates. But let there be no change by usurpation; for though this in one instance may be the instrument of good, it is the customary weapon by which free governments are destroyed." In spite of this warning, both the Executive and Judicial Departments have been guilty of continual usurpation for many years.

As early as 1894, Grover Cleveland violated Article IV, Section 4, of the Constitution by sending troops into Chicago to maintain order, not only without the request of the Illinois legislature or governor, but also against the governor's protest. Cleveland claimed he was protecting the U.S. Mail from interference by striking railroad employees. In later times, Presidents Eisenhower and Kennedy have likewise violated the same Article of the Constitution under the guise of enforcing the "law of the land." In fact, they enforced a court decree which at most was only the "law of the case."

"Executive Orders" in recent years have taken on the force of law without any act of Congress. The Peace Corps was created by executive order. Executive orders have been issued when there is no constitutional basis for such orders. They constitute so much usurpation.

Usurpation by the Supreme Court began with the school desegregation decision in 1954. In that decision, the court repudiated the separate but equal doctrine announced in Plessy vs. Ferguson in 1896, and in reliance upon psychology, not law, the Court in effect amended the Constitution by usurpation of the constitutional processes.

In the Steve Nelson case the court held that the Smith Act, and other federal statutes dealing with Communism, pre-empted the field and invalidated the Pennsylvania anti-subversive statutes, although the Smith Act plainly declared that such was not the intention of Congress.

The Conference of State Chief Justices held in Pasadena, California in August, 1958, charged the Supreme Court with acting without judicial restraint and with trying to constitute itself a third legislative body. To quote from the Report of the Chief Justices: "It has long been an American boast that we have a government of laws and not of men. We believe that any study of recent decisions of the Supreme Court will raise at least considerable doubt as to the validity of that boast."

"The extent to which the Supreme Court assumes the function of policy-maker is also of concern to us in the conduct of our judicial business. We believe that in the fields with which we are concerned, and as to which we feel entitled to speak, the Supreme Court too often has tended to adopt the role of policy-maker without proper judicial restraint."

The way the court has extended the meaning of the Preamble to the Constitution and the questionable Fourteenth Amendment confirms the Report of the Chief Justices. It has increased federal power at home and abroad far beyond the constitutional concept.

With all this usurpation Congress has done nothing. It could stop the effect of executive orders by cutting off the money supply. It could stop the unlawful invasion of states by taking a positive stand or by impeachment proceedings. It has the power under Article 3, Section 2, Clause 2, of the Constitution to regulate the appellate jurisdiction of the Supreme Court.

But for many years, Congress has most of the time assumed a servile attitude toward the other two branches of the Federal government and as of now it does not appear that those who represent the people and the states have any intention of restoring our constitutional Republic.

Under our Constitution, and the Way of Life provided by it, we have learned to produce the most of the best of everything known to history. Let us, therefore, not forsake it, but preserve and perpetuate it, not only for ourselves but also for our posterity.

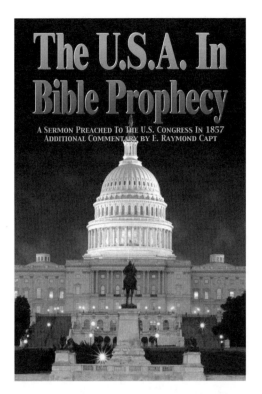

THE USA IN BIBLE PROPHECY

Revised & Expanded

Rev. F. E. Pitts

Did Christ know of this North American Continent? Sure he did. Did He know this great nation would be Christian from its beginning? Of course he did. Is it possible this greatest Christian super power of all time, known to Jesus Christ, was never mentioned, indicated, or foretold in the Bible? You will thrill as these questions are answered!

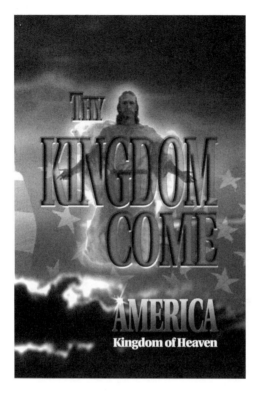

THY KINGDOM COME

(formerly TRACING THE ANCESTORS
OF GREAT BRITAIN AND AMERICA - THE ISRAELITES)

F. L. Hoffman

Tells the intriguing story of a people, the descendants of the twelve tribes of Israel that escaped from their Assyrians captors in 600 B.C. Christians today are puzzled that AMERICA, the greatest nation in history, is not mentioned in the Bible. This book will give the key to understanding prophecy, which will reveal the fact that the Old Testament prophets had much to say about America and its people.